Jail Pieces

and Other Poems

Couples' Troubles, Pests, Pirates

CAROLYN ANDERSON LONDON

Dedication

To my mother, Doris
Thank you for my love of poetry.

To Nanaw, Sallie Allen McCleary
Dear Lady, Survivor, Exemplar

To Robert Vernon Wirtz
Courageous fallen warrior

To Geordie with special thanks

To Alex, Lyal Henry, Lily, Cara, Lisa

Table of Contents

VII: Pirates

Introduction

Poetry is a breathing, living creature with varied faces and
moods.
Like us, it has imagination and longs to escape the bounds
that hold us down.

Sometimes it wants to be an eagle, master of the skies,
Swooping and soaring for the thrill
Of air currents thronging feathers
And for gladness in the might of talons.
It nests in high places,

Or a snail safely ensconced in chambered shell,
Or a whale breaching and piloting in endless seas,
Or a lovebird preening its mate,
Or a mourning dove ruing its fate,
Or a tiger striped and skulking in tall grasses,
Or a frog leaping and bellowing in its own pond.

But, most of all, it wants to be a wild horse
Galloping, mane and tail streaming, across open
Sunlit prairies in the joy of strength.

Poets reach to touch that flowing mane as it passes.

Dear Reader, these words and their melodies
Hope to reach you.

Section One

Jail Pieces

Introduction

The jail pieces derive from my experiences as a mental
health therapist in a detention center for adults.

The jail is a consuming place.
It grabs and won't let go.
It mocks with civility,
A mask over dread of chaos.
It is controlled by rule-bound people
Over rule-less people.

Petty dramas and serious cares are daily fare.
The cast changes, often rotates, but patterns stay the same.
Endings often are predictable but, sometimes, shocking
And raw.

Jail

Who am I working in this strange place
Where 20-somethings speak of death
Companionably, an accepted risk, with every dose,

Where a chemistry major brags of cutting drugs
And packing hot shots every 100th time,
And addicts cheer, praise him for random murders,

Where a 20-year-old girl, unconcernedly, points
To the one good vein she has left,
And that is between two fingers of her right hand,

Where a woman who twice set her home afire
Awaits trial for arson.
She became a living pyre,
Face and hands of molten skin
Congealed over bone.

Where a do-gooder tells
A suicidal young man his family
Would be better off without him.
They could collect benefits he cannot give them.

A place where every door is locked
Until medieval keys or unseen "Control" opens it.
Where steel doors grind closed,
And one is trapped in the sally port
With caught breath, bumping heart,
White-knuckling a radio.
Only "Control" can give release.

Where incessant radio calls, bodiless voices,
Echo throughout the jail,
"What's your 20? What's your 20? What's your 20?"

A place of man-down radios, lockdowns, take downs,
Spit-guard hoods and restraint chair,
An outsized infant seat,

Where toothbrushes become shanks,
And ink from stolen pens and paperclips
Becomes splotched tattoos,

A place that reeks of soured floor wax, sweat,
Desperation and, between crackdowns, fermenting
Orange peels of jailhouse hooch,

Where the warden's waffle evokes threats
Of hunger strikes or suicide,
And emboldened mice are fattened
By inmate feeding,

A place where a soul is but a number, no more, no less,
And chaplains give bad news, prayers and used
eyeglasses,

Where a killer awaits trial and muses,
That he, a self-named bad man, dived
Into a drive-by to take a bullet for a 3-year-old girl
And lost so much gut that food runs through him,
Without nourishment,

A place that leads to a judge
Who wields capricious sentences:
100 plus years for shoplifting,

A judge who apologizes to a baby killer
For the loss of his 6-week-old son
And sets him free with a clean record
To claim the new baby in utero.

Working in this strange place changes one,
Not always for the better.

Glitter Girl Dancer

It started young for her. First, it was Uncle Bob, Mother's dealer/pimp who claimed she owed him. Mother dared not oppose him, or perhaps she was too high to notice. Next, some of Mother's 'dates' craved something fresh and younger. Then there was the one, "He broke my brand new molar."

She blamed herself for the ones who grabbed and raped her at the schoolyard when the light had been shot out. "It was my fault. I wore that ruffled top with the pink roses and white kittens that I got for my birthday. My midriff was naked."

School did not go well. "I could not concentrate when I stayed up too late." The letters seemed to dance or sway. She drank and tripped on weekends. Soon, it was nearly every day if she could steal the money from Mother's purse. She got up too late to go to class and stopped bothering to go.

Instead, she picked up strangers until Uncle Bob offered her a job at his club. She needed to make money to support Mother whom the patrons jeered and called "Hag." Uncle Bob fired mother when he caught her fingers in the till and banned her from the club.

Now, she was the one who could wear cherry red taffeta and spangles. "It was almost like a real dance recital. I felt sparkling." She learned she could dance and sway like the letters. She could slink and dip and offer strategic views. Uncle Bob kept her supplied with drugs to keep her numb and compliant. When she fell from the stage, the patrons laughed and hooted and pushed her back up on the stage. The fall jarred her from her trance. For a moment, images of the schoolyard fell across her sooty eyes. It was the many sweaty hands that took her there. The patrons chanted, "Dance! Dance!" as she gyrated in her trance.

Once a do-gooder asked her, "What dreams do you have for your life?"

She paused and replied, "I can't remember."

Victoria Regina

Sent to decide if she were suicidal,
I saw her in the gloom of an iron cage,
This ruin of a suburban wife
With a queen's name
And three young sons to her credit.
Her dancer's body
Shivered and hunched in a paper
Gown that ripped in every movement
And shredded what was left of her dignity,
Exposing varied-colored bruises on her ribs and back.
One arm she could not raise
From the beating she had taken.

Mercy there was none
From the eyes of men
At a TV monitor
Who watched her every second
As she lay, chilled and coverless
On a naked concrete slab
Or perched on a stainless steel toilet.
There was no water at her sink
And she was thirsty, asking to drink.

I had known her in her previous sentence
When she spoke with clean eyes and hope
Of her plans for recovery
And reuniting with her sons.
It had seemed real and possible, then.
Now, the men wielded big, medieval keys
To open a steel door.

The glare of a hall light revealed her to me,
No sun, no window in her cage,
And she, behind bars, cringing.
Fear grabbed me
For her brokenness,
Her confused, disjointed comments
As she groped for understanding.
Detoxing, she tried to work out
Where she was: a hospital, a firehouse or jail.
Then, she thought she remembered me
And must be back in jail.

I saw her blackened eye, split cheek and swollen jaw,
But I went weak
When I looked into her eyes and saw,
Not those of a human,
But a dog.

Like bits of bone, she spit out her story:
Released, doing well,
By chance or fate
Ran into her dealer,
Scored some crack.
He put her to work on the street
Where she looked for friendly eyes
In the pockets of men.
She could not remember who beat her,
Her dealer or a john.

Property Owner

The stringy old man
Tottered into my office,
His head bobbing gently,
Hands with a tremor.

With hard work and parsimony,
He had paid for 3 rental properties.
They produced income, but he had lost track
Of the money. His family had 'managed' it
For the past three years since his wife died.

No one cooked or cleaned for him or visited.
It had been a long while since he'd had a real meal.
The church had slipped away
After the donations from his wife stopped.
"I figure they got enough of my money."

Sometimes his wife appeared to him,
Luring him to join her. This frightened him
Out of the house. The walls seemed to get closer,
And echoes of whispers seethed from those walls.
At times, he thought 'they' were after him
Or his money, but he couldn't say who 'they' were—
Thugs or maybe his family.

Hungry, he fled the house to pick through trash.
He had no money. The old work truck ran out
Of gas, and he abandoned it along the road.
Hiding in tall grass or among tree stumps,
He wandered across fields in a cold rain.
Drenched, chattering, hungry, weary and lost,
He took refuge in a barn, wrapped himself in insulation
He found there and slept.

The next morning, trailing insulation,
He crept to a farm house. No one was home
To answer his pleas. The door was locked.
With regret, he broke a window to enter
And use the phone to cry for help.
Someone saw and called the police
Who arrested him and took him to jail.
"I've never had so much as a parking ticket.
Even my old hunting dog had a license."

After a few meals and a few night's sleep
And a shower, his mind seemed clearer.
"How many weeks will it be until my trial?
When will the Public Defender come to talk with me?"
He didn't like the sound of the word 'indigent.'
The trial might end up being postponed
For 2 or 3 months after the trial date
If the P.D. were not allowed to represent him
Because he was a man of means.

He could have been bailed out at any time
If the family would have put up a small amount
Of his money.
They did not.

Booster

She was chef at a trendy restaurant,
A model of middle class solidity
And upward female mobility:
A condo and car payments,
Plush sectional sofas and executive,
Membership at a gym with juice bar
And two pug dogs with rhinestone collars,
Until cocaine kissed her nose
And sated every lust and love.

Shoplifting was an edgy game:
Luscious lingerie and uplift bras,
Hot CD's and diamond heart pendant,
Stiletto heels and designer denims,
Cashmere sweaters and credit cards,
Kited checks and pashmina shawls,

Until they caught her, ingloriously,
And leveled 50 charges.
Outraged, she declared the number
Was impossible.
The cops were clearing their books on her.

No priors. The judge slammed her with 115 years,
The number impossible to understand.
When the van unloaded her at prison,
She did the only thing left for a sane person to do:
A complete mental breakdown.
She disappeared into the care of the system.

Chemistry Major

He was well raised:
Genteel manners,
Look you in the eye
"Yes, Ma'am",
As though a righteous grandmother
Worn with cleaning other people's houses
Or airport toilets
Yet praised the Lord
And poured her prayers, her heart
And hope
Into him
And her life savings
Into his college tuition.

Cynically, I thought he did not waste
His education:
He used it to cut heroin
In the employ of his local dealer,
Although
He declared, "I never use the stuff."
"It will ruin your life," he preached.
Professor-like, he explained
To the group of addicts,
"Every one-hundredth bag
I make a hot shot, a death dose.
It increases business!
The word gets around:
We're selling the Good Stuff.

Knowingly the group
Nodded, smiled, slapped their desks
Then laughed,
Showing animation for the first time.
He had reached them
As I could not.

He resumed:
"Now, I know I am called
To be a Preacher."

The group hushed,
Giving him a chance,
But I, full of judgment
And moral superiority,
Was alarmed
To see
A golden light
Surrounding the base
Of his skull.
This light persisted
Despite
My blinking.

Billy

Billy was back
In the county jail,
Battered and looking older than his years.
We had made his discharge plans,
But the agency that had agreed to help
Discarded him on the street,
And he went back to drinking
Voraciously, eating little
And sleeping behind dumpsters.
Shelters were beneath him,
"They're full of thieves and often have no vacancies:
"They steal your shoes while you're sleeping."

Today, he was wild-haired, bruised and stiff,
Rocking in his chair,
As he tried to find a pain-free part to sit on.
He seemed sheepish at his failure
Or guarded, paranoid,
Without psych meds since release.
Even the VA had failed to serve him,
"Transportation problems."

I asked what he had been doing
While he was out.
The cold light in my office
Glinted on white and blonde stubble,
A few days unshaven,
And on his weak blue eyes
As he warmed to the story:
When they caught him,
He had fought determinedly, one against many,
With the police, the enemy.
He did not complain about their beating him,
Though they were known in that town for brutality.

He had stolen a police cruiser, embarrassed them,
And eluded them for five hours,
Because, he explained,
"I was on patrol."

Reading doubt on my face
Or in my questions about "patrol",
He stiffened to his military bearing
And rebuked me:
"I've got the younger guys
In the dorm calling me "Sarge".
Billy was reputed to have served
His country in Viet Nam.
He was old enough and a veteran,
And I thought it might be true:
He had snapped closed, shut down,
When Viet Nam was mentioned.
He did not want to talk about that.

Billy had twice proposed marriage to me
In his courtly manner and soon repeated his offer
As I declined again.
He confided, "I need a good woman
To take care of me,
And you look like you might be a good woman."
His mother had died, and his sister burned out.
"Billy," I thought, "you probably do need
Some good woman,"
Unlikely though it seemed,
"But, first, let's get you back on meds,"
As I pushed his name to the top of the referral list.

Some weeks later, I saw him in the dorm,
Standing straight-backed, clean shaven, hair trimmed,
And asked how he had been doing.
Looking frail but unbending as ever,
He countered, "I did not ask to see you
Because you should help those
Who need your help."

Baby Killers

The judge let the baby killer go,
And so, the killer had no dirty record
To smear his chances
For custody
Of the next baby, then, in utero.

The judge, basking in the glow
Of self-admiration
For his interpretation
Was taken in by the killer's story
Of brain-damaged plight
And oppressed ethnicity.
The judge's words of sympathy
For the killer
Ran in the local paper.

I had listened for weeks
To the killer's demands of entitlement
And boasts of lawyer's plans
For custody suit
For the unborn baby his wife carried,
Conceived four weeks after the first was born
And two weeks before the baby boy was killed.
I had seen the killer's kingdom of comfort
Set up in his privileged single cell.
He was deemed too much
At risk to be in general population.
I had listened to his insistence
On the injustice of his confinement
For "what had happened"
And his predictions he would be freed
Because of sympathy.

The pregnant wife played her role of innocence
As week after week she recounted to me
The tortures her husband had inflicted
On the baby's body that bore old bruises
And cracked bones at six weeks of age.
The baby was underfed and failed to thrive.
Her anger flashed at the nuisance
Of caring for a new baby.
She insisted she had a right to sleep
And that her meds made
Her sleep too soundly
Too feed him,
And she feared her husband, never
Protested his throwing the baby, repeatedly,
In games of indoor football with his friend,
Never protested his clutching the baby
By the throat against the wall
And letting go to watch him fall,
Repeatedly,
Never protested his sliding the baby
Down his lap, repeatedly,
To slam his head on the floor.

She repeated these horrors to me
That she supposedly was too asleep to see.
She claimed to be a prisoner,
Tried once to escape but
Could never find a time when husband slept
Or left the house.

She took a plea of felony
Child endangerment
And promised to give up the new baby
For adoption as soon as it was born.
She reneged on her promise
And got away with it.
Convincing the states attorney
That one is too pitiful to prosecute, works.

The friend is the only one
Serving time, ten years
For his pass receptions.
With good time, he may do five or six.
He prides himself on the life-
Saving mission
Of his blood donations.

Arrogant

Moonhead "Arrogant"
Swaggered down the hall
As if he were ready
To be a big presence in the jail.

He swung his striped shoulders
In cadence to his ever-so-casual
Denim legs,
Plastic sandals flapping
In ungainly flopping.

He was little more than a boy, a first-timer,
Pale, a skinhead whose bold tattoo
Covered his temple and side of head.
It announced "Arrogant,"
To his new world,
Waiting to show him his place.

The shaded side
Of his lunar skull
Partly hid a large message
Or threat, "Vicious."

Cuddles

"I grew up in a brothel," Cuddles said.
Reading concerned shock on my face, he countered,
"It wasn't so bad. I did alright there. Where else could a boy
Have so many ladies, almost like second moms?
My mom gave me a present for my thirteenth birthday,"
He waited for my, "What was that?"
"It was a woman she bought for me for my birthday."

Cuddles told me about a ride with his wife and two children.
They had seen a second dead deer at the same place.
"A fawn. Children should not see things like that," he mourned.
"I called the county over and over until I got them to put up a sign
To save lives:
DEER CROSSING- with a jumping deer on it!" he beamed.

In the dorm, Cuddles tore the plug from the shared hot pot,
Put water in a foam cup along with the naked wires and his penis
And plugged it into the outlet.
After this, the CO's put him in isolation
So that the dorm could have another hot pot.

Then he tied a string tightly around his penis.
After some days, it swelled and festered.
Armed with tweezers, the doctor picked pieces of rotting string
Out of Cuddles' inflamed penis.
How, or if, it would heal the doctor could not say.

Isolation Man

In the local rag
The warden bragged
He was there when it happened.
I would not brag
Of being unaware and unable to prevent it,
But he may have been easing his conscience:
It would have looked worse if the paper
Said they had to track him down
On the golf course for comment.

The warden labeled him "a troublemaker"
And accused him, "We moved him
Twenty-three times,"
In the few months he was held there.
Again, I would not brag
About the lack of suitable celling for him.
He was twenty-two years old,
His blonde, pale and lean body
Already turning blue
When they cut him down.

It all began with a frantic call
For scissors, locked up like all sharps,
Then the call for Medical department
To bring their bag
And the All-Available-Officers call.
It was a stampede, but a practiced one.
I was ordered to stay in the Medical Treatment Room
So that it could remain unlocked
And to hold his chart in my hands,
Give it to no one, guard
It with my life.

They laid him in the hallway.
The head nurse straddled him.
She sweated and pumped and beat on his chest
With demonic endurance
For twenty-five minutes until the EMT's came
With a gurney to take him away.

Nothing worked,
Not the oxygen, not the pumping,
Not the beating life back into him.
They all knew it was for nothing,
That he was dead
When they cut him down,
But no one could call him dead
Until the doctor came to pronounce him
And record the time.

Later, the nurses told me his neck was not broken.
This meant he had strangled slowly.
It could have taken up to twenty minutes.
He may have been conscious
Most of that time.
He had tied his hands behind his back
Before he jumped. He meant it.

Outside the jail, it was a late spring day,
Pleasant, offering promise of life.
His one-year-old daughter
May have been playing at home
While he, not thirty feet away from us
In the Medical Treatment Room,
Strangled slowly behind iron bars
And a steel door.

The family refused to claim the body,
Avoiding disposal cost.
Three weeks later, their letter came,
Announcing intent to sue for negligence
And wrongful death.

Deena

Red hair curled to her shoulder,
A pretty face, slightly sagging
And body spread past nubile tone,
No longer fit for stripping,
She served behind the bar,
Drinks and drugs past remembering,
Guided young girls through the mazes
And lent an ear to scams of any patron.

Something drove her from West Virginia.
Was it the uncle or step-father who shamed her
Or a chance, a hope of something better
Than toothless faces and babies on her apron strings?

Instead, she conceived her own scheme,
Diverting credit applications from mailboxes
Into generous presents for her friends.
"They're never for myself," she bragged.
"It can't be wrong to make people happy,
And banks will eat the losses."

"The kidnap charges are bogus," she insisted.
"I cared for the child four years
While the mother drugged and hooked
Until she turned me in for spite.
I would not, could not buy the child."

"My troubles," she declared, "are not my fault.
They're caused by waking one morning to find
The john had died sometime in the night
In my bed! I slept with a dead man!"
Her horror was beyond reckoning but not her plan:
"Some doctor needs to say it's not my fault."

In extradition, two deputies bent to her pleas
And let her use a diner bathroom
While they had coffee.
She escaped through a bathroom window
To the woods and towns of her youth.
It was a long year before she was caught again
On some new offense or outstanding warrant.

Torch

She came into the jail, small but shackled,
Empty eyed yet intent on arson.
Some voice in the voracious orange
Heathen flames, their roaring
Chant of cleansing freedom,
Lured her with certain recognition,
An infernal greeting or incantation
To a winged victory shrieking of immolation.

An acolyte, she nurtured flames
Sacred in their upward reaching
To a heaven of her making, disorderedly divine.
She kindled and courted streaks
Of pulsing flamelets to magnify
And erupt into an all-seeing, forgiving deity.
Mind seething, she transfigured into a mighty being
Reigning, swaying with the flames,
All powerful in her apogee.
A searing Salome in veils of fire she danced
With demons in the shadows of her skull.

A forgiving judge set her free
To roam the streets, mental
Balance elusive as sprigs of fire in rain.
She reappeared at the jail,
Her molten face congealed in lava trails,
No shackles this time,
Not enough flesh for chains to cling.
From that cave, her voice faintly moaned
Something like words.

Tattoo Maker

He sat before me and studied my eyes
As he pulled one leg of his knee pants
Far up his thigh and then the other
To show me his handiwork.
He praised what a great tattoo artist he is,
"It is an art, not a craft, and it is my life."

From his caved cheeks, he watched my eyes,
Seeking a reaction of shock or even attraction
In his effort to control or intimidate me.
I calculated a reaction. If I appeared scared or looked away
In embarrassment, he would count it as a win.
The story would make the rounds of the other inmates.
Instead I stared him down, ruing that I am not more clever,
And hoping he would look away first.

His next gambit was to start to hike up his striped shirt.
Asserting control, I told him that would not be necessary.
Next, he pointed to blurred stains on his wasted arms.
His stringy legs were smeared with ugly blotches
In which he took great pride. And so, we parried
Until he learned he would not get sleep meds.

Bored, he turned to the role of sage advice giver.
He lectured me about the skill he showed in making tattoos.
He quizzed me, "Where is the worst place to get a tattoo?"
And answered his own question, "At a tattoo party."
He and other artists would be too high
To use sterile techniques.
"Sometimes I would run out of gloves or stick myself
Or share inks between customers.
"It's a good way to get AIDS," he prophesied.

Driver

He killed them
On their wedding night:
Speeding, center-line confused,
Brakes screaming, crash exploding, rolling,
Shards of glass and steel,
Shattering lights and lives,
Blood streaks on white gown, bits of lace,
Alcohol, too much to remember.

Eighteen, birthday in jail,
He passed from minor to adult,
Barely old enough to be a criminal.
At first, disbelief:
Can what the newspapers call me be true?
Me – a killer?

Contrition, brief:
I deserve to be punished.
Scared, innocent of jail ways,
He was not suicidal:
I've got a lot of life left to live!

Two weeks later, in the halls, swaggering,
In step with other inmates,
He crowed, *Jail is almost like camp*
Without canoes or crafts
But lots of cool dudes to learn from.
It's the longest I've been sober since age thirteen.

Be boasted, knowingly,
I cut off my hair
So no one can grab me or hold me.
Denial:
It was an accident after all.

Calculation:
My lawyer can get a deal.
They'll say I can be saved
Because I'm so young.
I won't be here for long.

Wrapper

She seemed to be a likeable girl
For a murderer.
Polite, well-raised, she could be imagined
As a daughter.
Her brown hair rich with vitality
Swirled and wrapped about her shoulders
As if dancing, keeping time to her gestures.

She wondered about her baby boy
Given up at birth.
Had it been the right thing to do
And did she miss him enough
To mean she should have kept him?

There had been her bed-bound mother,
The interminable disease,
The mouth increasingly demanding,
The lack of relief and the lost car, the freedom given up.

She talked about spending the last years
Of her life in prison.
She was not streetwise
To build a cover story of innocence
In case the counselor were called to testify.
She told a story
Of a tumor fattening in her brain,
Like an overfed chick refusing to fledge.
It would press on her respiratory center,
Killing her in six years time.

Sadly, she dwelled on the life
She would not have
Before the end,
Yet she said she was not sorry
For her crime
Though she knew it was wrong
To smash the pillow into her mother's
Quarreling face, the nasty grimace
That pushed her patience
Beyond its limit.
She forced it there until the struggling stopped.
Her strength surprised her.

She wondered what it would be like for her,
Running out of air
Like her mother.
She had trouble sleeping,
Waking panicked without air.
Then she complained
The jail water was too harsh
On her cream and butter skin.

She did not mention to me
That she had wrapped her mother's body
Over and over in layers of food wrap
And stuffed it in a closet.

Weeper

Exploding into tears, she dropped into a chair
And fidgeted her fingers as she spluttered,
"Was it really seventeen times?"
Reading confusion on my face, she demanded,
"Did I really stab him seventeen times?
That's what the newspaper says!"

"Two weeks ago I told the doctor
 We drink and fight every night.
Something is going to happen.
The doctor said go to rehab.
He didn't understand.
Who would care for my dogs?
The old one needs meds and massage
Five times a day.
No one will take care of them the way I do!"

"They took my dogs I don't know where
Or what has happened to them.
I used my one phone call to ask my sister-in-law
To take them, but she hung up on me!
What will happen to them?"

"I want to go home to my country
So my family can visit me.
They can't afford air fare, and they don't write.
Maybe they've forgotten me!
I gave up my family and my country to marry him.
Then, he would not let me have children.
He always ridiculed my body.
Everything I did was wrong. Nothing satisfied him.
Twenty years, I saw my family only twice,
But I loved him!"

She paused to sob again and again.
"Twenty years of my life I gave him,
And I wanted children. I'll never have them!
I'll have to give up twenty more, I guess, in prison.
Someone asked me was it worth it?
I don't know.
The doctor should have prevented it.
After I am sentenced, my lawyer will try for extradition
So that my family can visit me.
I'll never see them here."

"No one will visit me since he is dead,
But I miss him!
He announced he would divorce me
After all I did for him!
Twenty years I took his cruelty.
He said he wanted to date again.
I thought he meant other women
Younger and prettier than I am.
No, he said, he wanted to date other men."

"After that, I don't remember what happened
Until there were lights shining on me and sirens
From police cars!
Who will take care of my dogs?"

Turkey Neck

A scrawny man, chinless,
His crepe-skin wattle
Rippled on his neck,
Waffling as he dodged meaning
With his words.
Anxiety was his issue,
But that would get him no meds.
They were not within budget
And can be addictive.
I skirted the system to refer him
For an antidepressant for calming effect,
Although it could take weeks to kick in.

He feared the hit-listed inmates-
Co-defendants or their friends,
But more than these men, he feared
Demons or shadows, memories of the crime
Skulking in his skull
Or erupting behind his eyes.
Asleep or waking, they confounded him
In terror and in sweaty whimperings in his sleep.
He suffered flashes of an old man beaten to death,
A tractor and a barn.

He claimed not to remember what troubled him,
And I was willing to listen to symptoms, not confessions.
Then he admitted he did not dare to remember:
"They'll kill me if I tell," while he wept
His possible innocence.

Drunk, he had hung out with 2 or 3 men.
He had no idea what they planned.
Maybe he took part; maybe he didn't.
His answer lay locked within him.

Now when panic attacks would constrict him,
He would threaten suicide
Until he gained the ear of a therapist.
His threats increased
As the dreaded trial drew near.
Then, to avoid the trial,
He sprang for a deal
That was no deal at all- 55 years,
Possible parole in 40 years.
When questioned, he replied:
"What's the difference? I'll never get out alive.
Will they hunt me when we all get to prison?"

Victor

Victor's love was the lading of ships,
The scent of the harbor
And the allure of places he'd never see,
The sounds of accents unlike his family.
He'd risen to gang leader over 17 men.
He relished their company
Now that he was the big man,

But he loved smoking 'greens,' PCP, even more.
It took him to unknown places
And eased his anxiety or so he said.

He lectured me: "There is a right way
And a wrong way of off-loading ships.
You gotta figure what is most important to do first.
You gotta remember the numbers and aisles
And keep the weight balanced,
But now I can't remember the numbers;
Like which comes first, second, third and so on.
The guys laughed when I took to writing them down
And called me 'old man'.
One day, me and the guys got so high
We dumped a crane into the harbor.
We snowed the company, claimed it was an accident,
And we got away with it."

What lost him the job was getting caught
Smoking greens in the hold.
"It was like I fell into a bad dream and got trapped.
I couldn't figure my way out."
He panicked, shouting and banging
And combating those who came to help.

Next, he tried construction work
Until $1200 worth of tools were stolen from his truck.
He'd lost the keys to lock the chest.
Stealing tools came next: "You gotta have tools to work."
Arrest followed: "I was just walking around with this stuff.
I couldn't remember where I left my truck.
I forgot I broke into that same van the week before."
Then came odd jobs: "I'm pretty good with my hands."

By that time, he'd lost his wife, his house,
The Lazy Boy and the dog.
He'd stolen it back from his wife,
But it ran away, and he could not find it.

"My P.O. violated me because I didn't show up
A few times. I had things to do.
Then, my aunt wanted her grass cut before it rained.
You know, family comes first.
It's not fair to go to jail
For cutting my aunt's grass.

Phobia Muridae

It was cold in the fall, and mice were burrowing into the jail for warmth and food fed to them by inmates. My office, a disused mattress storage closet with no ventilation, was in the Med-Iso corridor where the crazies and contagious were celled. I tried to focus on paperwork despite the fact that I had seen a mouse at the end of the corridor, trying to get into the nasty bosses' office. "Good," I thought, "but a rat would be better."

I had asked two passing CO's and the Chaplain if they had seen the mouse, but they said not and hurried on, yet I knew it was only too real. It had disappeared. Next, I asked Jose, a hall trustee and information source with other inmates. He would know the whereabouts of the mouse. Reading my apprehension, Jose gallantly reassured me. "Don't worry, Miss. If I see it, I'll stomp on it for you." I caught myself from saying, "Don't do that!" I thought it unlikely, and I did not want to reject his good intention, although relying on an inmate would be a role reversal. I thought, "Who is supposed to be helping whom? I am the mental health therapist. I am supposed to be a model of adjustment and stability. I am supposed to be an authority figure."

The screaming in our corridor made it hard to concentrate on paperwork. For two days and two nights, Priscilla of the loud lungs and relentless mouth continued to bellow lewd invitations, "I'll take you on and your brother. I'll take on anybody and outlast you all!" Even inmates had asked me to get her medicated, but she had refused. Forced medication is illegal in this state.

Cuddles, one of the crazies whose cell was next to my office was telling stories of King Arthur and the Knights of the Roundtable. As I would pass by, I heard the stories get weirder and more convoluted as the evening wore on, but

Cuddles had accomplished what no one else could do. Priscilla shut up to listen.

With great relief, I turned back to the pile of paper work. Some sixth sense caused me to look below the projecting legs of my swivel chair on which my feet rested. Beneath my very feet, a mouse sat expectantly looking up at me with its beady eyes! My screaming startled the mouse. It scuttled to the door, ajar. Terrified, it tried to claw its way under the door, but it was too fat. Desperate, it was able, finally, to squeeze through the slit of the door ajar.

Trembling, I realized I could not stay in that chair forever. I was going to have to walk where the mouse had trod even though I would need to throw out my shoes. Hours later, when the shift would end, the CO's would come looking, not for me, but for their keys and radio required for the count. Steeling myself, I tiptoed to the door and slammed it behind me, hoping I could think of a reason never to enter the office again. Then I remembered I had left a pile of medical charts on the desk. After several deep breaths, I retrieved the charts.

Fumbling with the keys, I heard Cuddles interrupt his stories and ask me, "Miss, what was all that screaming about?"

My shaking voice betrayed me, "It was a mouse!" Skeptically he questioned, "All that screaming about a mouse?"

"Yes!" I insisted with whatever dignity I could summon.

Calaboose*

A Song In Four Parts

Cellie:
Man inna calaboose
Ain' getting' loose.
Ain' no time soon
He be onna caboose
O' las' train leavin' this town.

Con:
Ya thinkin' ya better'n me,
Livin' in yer big house onna hill,
But I built yer walls, yer chimneys an' cellar,
Yer house wit' all them columns.
Fer ma labor I got near nothin'
'Cept all the dirt I could shovel,
And whenna sun's settin',
Ya drinkin' yer wine an' yer whiskey,
Lookin' downna valley
At them shacks inna holler
Countin' yerself better.

Mr. Judge:
I don' wan' no 'scuses
Fer doin' yer evil.
Law say man done in
Means someone done wrong,
An' ya gonna pay.
Ain' no paycheck
Ya gonna pay wit'
'Cause ya done the crime,
Ya gonna do the time.

Ya gonna break rock.
Ya gonna break stone.
Ya broke yer mama's heart
An' laid her low inna grave
An' made yer daddy dead 'shamed.

Mr. Warden: I got ma eye cocked yer way
An' ma thumb on ma shotgun
An' a pistol on ma hip.
Ma finger's huggin' that trigger
Jes' waitin' fer ya to stray.
I'll pepper ya good
'Til the blood run gray.
Ya troublemakin' from a day
Ya was hatched from some Hell's egg
Inna state o' the misbegotten,
But ya'll be doin' hard time, ain' no soft time
here,
'Cause crime it don' pay, not in ma state.

Mr. Judge: I say man done in
Means ya done wrong.
Ya inna pokey
'Thout no smokes.
All that drinkin' an' cussin',
All that smokin', wit' fast women runnin',
Keepin' that bad company,
Ya 'come a gamblin' man,
Heart turnna stone
Cold as that river
Never float ya home agin.

Con: Mista Judge, ya sits on yer butt bones
Up on yer throne
Wit' yer robe an' yer gavel
Judgin' me down,
Like some false pagan idol.
I'm a man jes' like ya, only better.
I live hard times
Wit' no hope fer no future
An' ma belly groanin' wit' hunger
An' peoples squashin' me down.

Pure meanness keepin' me strong
Wit' the will ta go on
'Til I meet ya an' play ya hand in Hell.
Yer rules is fer fools
Whenna joker's the king
An' getting' away is the ace,
Whenna deuces run wild
Like guards wit' they's guns an' clubs.

Mista Warden, ma day be comin'
Sure as that settin' sun
Kickin' me loose
From this ole calaboose,
N'ole big house
Holdin' me fer long.

Ain' ma fault
Pretty women's talkin' ain' true.
Whatsa man ta do?
Gotta git what he can
When it's ther fer.
I seen pokey, an' I seen stir.
I done me a stretch or two.
Ain't no pick I cain' swing
An' no hammer I cain' ring.
Don't tear me down none
'Cause ma time ain' be long
I'll be singin' ole calaboose song
Onna freight train outta this town.

Then I'll be sayin',
Mista Judge, ya done me wrong.
Ya cin keep yer pokey
'Cause I'm mean lucky
An' leavin' yer town.
Ain' no welcome
Fer no travelin' man onna run.

There's mud on ma shoe
An' dust in ma heart, hang so low,
An' ma road's bin long
An' all so wearisome.
Ma ankle's skinned raw wit' them shackles
Like a hawg hung fer bleedin',
'Cause a man here's worth less
Than a pig fer the stickin'.
I'm eatin' last week's beans,
An' them guards is sure mean.
They's dog's teeth is keen sharp,
An' they's bites worser than they's bark.
Them dogs is growlin',
An' coyote's howlin'
Atta moon ain' save no man's soul.

'Though them dogs chews ma leg,
Belly shackles never maken' me beg.
Ya cin chain a man up,
But ya cain' never break 'im
Unless-en he lets 'em
Take him down in his soul.

Ain' no moon bright 'nough
Naw chain gang long 'nough
Ta keep this man down.
Then night birds is singin' ma song,
An' ma hearts a-liftin'
Ta rise up wit' they's wingin'
An' be free.

I'll be crossin' the Jordan
When I'm makin' that border,
No dogs houndin' me,
No guards poundin' me,
No sheriff, no police trackin' me down,
Ain' no place they be findin' me.

I'm gonna prowl like a polecat
An' swoop like an owl,
Roll like a river
An' lose 'em like a wild goose.
I'll be quicker'n a snake
When I'm makin' ma break
From this ole calaboose
An' yer rotten ole town.

I'll be raisin' the ante
An' leavin' yer shanty.
I'll see yer hand
An' call yer plan
'Gainst keepin' me in this place.
Straight flush is my cards,
An' ma fist it's rock hard.
Ma will cain' be broke,
Got ma own ace o' spades
An' a shank fer a thank ya.

Then, ain' no preacher man save 'em
Whenna smoke pourin' down,
An' flames reachin' fer heaven.
Then them dogs be runnin',
An them guards be gunnin'.
Then they'll be knowin'
I said ma goodbye.

*This is an imagined poem of events in the early
1900s in the rural South.

Section Two

Couples' Troubles

Introduction: Couples' Troubles

These pieces derive mainly from counseling couples in my
work in private practice.

The daily rub of rock wills
On blunted hearts
And misplaced hopes
Grind dreams to dust.

Couples' Story

I.
He impresses.
She undresses.
Lured by anarchic impulses
In bones, nerve ends, they wed.
Soon trapped, they resent.
He annoys; she laments.
Malcontents, neither can recall
The reason they gave their all.
Some fleeting fancy had been the trigger.
Over foggy fantasies they linger
And wonder how
Could they have been so wrong,
Or is there any remedy
For their mutual malady?

II.
They part: boozing, spending benders,
Diets, exercise and makeovers
To present a facile face
To any prospective mates.
They contend over real estate,
Music albums or who gets the dog,
While children challenge.
Angry, sad or confused,
They shuttle between probing
Parents who demand the news
Of mommy's latest loser
Or daddy's tramp.
This year they can't
Afford oboe lessons or summer camp.

III.
Divorce seems the shining glory
For their dreary story.
Patient friends or therapists
Groan through pity
Sessions and confessions.
She alleges; he admits.
Lawyers pick the bones.
Trial lovers come and go.
Between drama and contention,
Jealousy and mistaken hopes,
New loves somehow lack the luster
The first one had engendered
Until they both discover
The most enduring lover is the self.

Dumpers

(Or, At least the next one won't
stuff smelly socks between sofa cushions.)

I.
She's lured him to sessions
With promises to fix problems.
True, he snores and watches sports.
He's got a temper, bald spot and a paunch,
But he works all day though he likes his beer too much.
"I do enough," he says. She wants more
And thinks she's found him,
Twice divorced, but his kids are nearly grown.

The exes are witches, out only for money
To sparkle their nails, not paying school lunches.
Expensive hairdos, personal trainers, the latest shoes
Consume his child-support payments.

Unwary therapist, don't be lured in.
She's here for help to dump him.

II.
She's got it planned,
New apartment already rented.
She and new man changed e-mail addresses.
Who gets her kids is the issue:
Will they like their new daddy
And make friends in new school?

Both men soon question, "Am I a fool
Or just her tool?
What's it going to cost me
If she bails first?
Then who gets stuck with the bills?"
But, a done-up lady doesn't come cheap:
A trim figure, hoop earrings and bottle-blonde hair,
Rosy pink nails. A little love can be dear.

Mates

I.
Creeping Boredom
Numbs the skull.
One says, "Let's experiment!"
The other, hurt, assents:
Swapping, three- or foursomes,
Bondage, leather, punishment,
Chains and whips, spikey collars,
Piercings become divertissements.
When sordid is the order,
The darker side seems brighter,
And cruelty seems kind,
Until confused in paled enthusiasm,
Self-respect, bruised and lacking,
They regret bartered innocence.

II.
When titillation turns to squalor,
One licks boots, becomes a crawler.
The other brandishes a whip,
Finds that mastery ignites a passion
Long a-slumber. Secret wounds,
Relish and resentment they heap on the side
With helpings of pummeled pride.
Warm eyes harden into ice berg
Lettuce sauced with degradation.
From their frolicsome rites
They glean lessened satisfaction.
They root aground in search of truffles
And feed paucity of hope
In the trough of humiliation.

III.
They recruit beginners,
New flesh to use
With wills to break
And spirits to taint.
They find the tension gratifies
In knowing the loathing
Their victims are yet to feel
For their bodies or their souls.
The anger they soon wield
On hapless others
Is venom they soon will spread.
Spite casts daggers from their eyes
As they lie or promise pleasure
When corruption is the measure.

Flirt

I.
She's a flirt.
He feels hurt,
And, confused, he asks,
"What is enough
To keep her home?"
She is heedless
Of his complaints,
Claims he's jealous for no reason.
She simply craves attention,
But she is restless
For what she's missing.
It may be out there waiting.
Soon she finds a taker
Though he's married with children.

II.
He claims his wife lacks
Understanding and neglects him,
Dotes on her job
Or the children.
There are thrills
Of secrets, kept,
And trysts, illicit.
There arc missing hours,
Calls, whispers.
There is grief and suspicion.
It's a stale story, frankly boring,
Of trust broken, drama, foreboding
And, perhaps, caustic reconciliations
Haunted by recriminations.

III.
"It's for the children," they say
Who are resented
For needs presented,
Who ponder what they've done wrong
To cause such unhappiness.
Arguments belie formal faces.
Outings are tedious, bothersome.
It takes the children so very long
To grow up and end their parents' sentence.
When, at length, they escape,
The parents find they are alone
In the end with each other.
The search for lovers is taxing.
TV is more relaxing.

Liars

I.
There are liars in the mirror
And in some men's eyes
Assuagers of desires.
In some are talons, in other's guile
And in women's vaunted wares,
The makings of their despair.

Led by urges, merciless,
They seduce and produce
Jagged images of hurt.

Meanwhile, the mirror ages,
Cracks or leers in solemn glazes,
As silver on the back crazes
Then returns, eye for eye,
The same lies.

II.
Unwary beholders grieve to find
The charms that lured
Are in their minds.
If hearts have teeth or claws,
The smiles that seethe
From mirror frames
Betoken winning games
When lashes of eyes contrive
To entrap in winsome gaze
And connive in grappling ways
The torments that they crave
Or lurk in liars' eyes
Then deny in bewildered state
The mirror of their plays.

Butterflies

I.

He speaks to her of butterflies
And how he cannot resist
The aura of loveliness
Or how she is but one of such
And should not grieve so much,
That his adoring eyes
May hold lust,
But it is not the same as touch.
Says he, "I would be loath
To steal the dust
From oh-so fragile wings
Though butterflies have neither heart
Nor soul and are but beings
Inclined to feed on dross or leavings."

II.

"You should not think yourself so grand
To merit the only attentions of a man.
Brightly-colored wings soon fade
And, tattered in hot winds, break
Or, chilled by indifference, wilt
And have no one to appreciate
Their shattered state.
In their brief span
Flight itself escapes."
She consoled herself that the ache
She feels might be beginnings
Of heart or soul.
Said she, "Where else can I find
One who charms with his poetic mind?"

Standoff

I.
He's got a nasty mouth,
And she's got spite.
He harasses;
She embarrasses
And picks a lover.
He tends to hover
To thwart her straying.
She perfects the art of sneaking
But leaving trails to distress him.
He's bewildered
Why his mouth's a problem.
He's only unloading stress.
He berates; she learns to hate.
It's a stalemate.

II.
Standoff is an art form
For the forlorn.
They reach a stasis
Of frozen faces.
They court a distance
Set in grimaces, graceless.
Reconciliations are baseless
For neither seems willing,
And both are too rigid to change.
He keeps dumping and denigrating.
She keeps score of his offenses
And seeks another lover,
'Though she soon discovers
There are worse ones to uncover.

Feuding Duo

I.
Grit in the eye, sand in the heart,
They rasp on one another,
Grate and irritate.
They commiserate
With loyal friends
Whose reward is to be bored
And who speculate
How long can this go on,
Who then reassess
The success of their domestic-ness
Or marvel how can this couple
Be so dysfunctional,
Secrets bared bring awkwardness,
Less respect and stilted jests.

II.
Friends feel compelled
To dissuade outrageous
Escapades, then repelled,
Long for truces
Between these feuders
They hope will repent
And relent to use
Remnants of common sense
To restore good order
From pointed accusations
Or useless recriminations.
Then, patience spent,
They come to resent
The ever-present lament.

III.
They wonder how could these fools
Have been their friends?
They divide over which side
To back in this drama.
He sides with one,
She with the other.
Soon, they argue
And contend over dinner.
She sees victim; he sees loser or winner.
The contagion spreads
From one home to others'.
Meanwhile, the feuders
Take satisfaction their distress
Is shared in commonness.

Organ Grinder's Monkey

I.
She is the organ grinder's monkey,
And into a slot of mind he drops
Coins, cheap words of undying love.
She, needy and delighted, supports him
'Though he disdains toil
And mocks her to explain:
"My work is watching TV sports,"
And eating all the refrigerator contains,
While he complains, "There is never enough."
He grinds the crank harder and faster:
A second job to please her master.
He sneers how easily women are controlled:
"Words of love will keep them dancing.
They are silly girls," or monkeys prancing.

II.
He doles out permission to speak or visit
Then texts or calls to interrupt
Lest someone convince her
His scorn is not caring,
And his using is not love.
She has no money for coffee or gas
And subsists on promises and potato chips.
Her family doles out pity and twenties
And preaches, "You choose to be a victim."
Her friends have desisted from warnings.
His past is thieving and preying on women.
No jobs are worthy of his talents.
This time he got lucky
And chained an eager monkey.

Yoke Mates

Pandora's box might be made for her
According to husband's estimation.
She finds his constant berating aggravating.
He fights her resistance to subjugation
And finds her lacking in remorse
For resenting his chastisement.

She calls him "chicken little"
For his frequent catastrophizing.
She wishes he'd take up mountain climbing
Or sky diving for obvious reasons.
Extreme skiing is another option in icy season.

They battle on in mutual condemnation.
He seeks to break her.
She spends his money to bait him.

Section Three

Pests

Introduction to Section Three: Pests

If only they could speak...

Rodentia

Professor Pestis:

Gnawers, settle down for class. Do not chew one another's tail or bat it. We must respect each other. Listen to me and learn from one who has avoided crafty traps and lived to the age of canes. You have much to learn before you stray on your own. You will learn that the world is not all cheese for you to savor. Indeed, there are insidious traps out there. Beware peanut butter, the invention of evil men! Where there is peanut butter, there are deadly springs attached. Shun seeds in neat trays. Young ears should not hear what happens to those who are lured in to easy meals.

Among their failings, humans have never thanked us for cleaning after them. We eat their crumbs and clean out their pantries. They hoard far more than they can eat at one time. Their leftovers serve a better purpose feeding us than souring in their hoardings. Their selfishness has no limits, and their brooms are quick.

Cunningly, they have hidden lightning strings in their walls to kill us. Those who bite lightning wires do not return to the nest. It were safer for us to make our nests under garden pots. Avoid sheds where they hoard grass seed to tempt us but keep tools with sharp points.

Men have sworn a war against our kind. They employ armies of vicious pointed-ear fiends to patrol their alleys. They are not satisfied to kill our friends and families. No, they must first torture us and relish our terror. Few escape their sword claws and razor teeth.

Our country kin seem to lead an idyllic life, fields of grain and sacks in barns. Alas, these friendly-seeming barns harbor more of the same hissing fiends. Round towers, laden with grain, crush those who tunnel into oblivion. Everywhere, life is perilous no matter how hard we try to be inconspicuous.

There is nothing to be learned from our fat-tailed cousins, tree rats. They chatter and complain and accuse incessantly. They have nothing on their minds but acorns. Like men, they, too, are hoarders, yet, like men, they often forget where they have buried their true treasures.

Hawks may whistle appealingly, while owls always ask the same question, "Who, who?" This means, "Who will be our next meal?" Fox may grin at you before he licks your blood from his chops. Beware raccoon! His mask covers dirty secrets, and his hands are stained dark despite constant washing. Do not ask why.

Ignore rabbit. He mumbles through a mouthful of grass and weeds, and we have the same enemies. Even war machines of rolling blades assail us!

Do not argue with rats. They are crime lords. Agree with what they say, then bow and back away slowly.

And so, Gnawers, never run in the open. Instead, scurry along the edges of walls. Chew escape holes in advance. Stay grey. Be inconspicuous, but invisible would be better.

Mosquitoes

Memo to: Humans
From: Semper Sallow, Dir. Of PR
CC: Major Blight, Crowd Control
Re: Annual Blood Drive

Blood is good. That buzzing you hear is a thank you for your donations, and welts serve as your receipts. Whirring wings are courtesy of Mass Transportation Div. We travel in throngs to where humans wait to offer oblations.

We are grateful, and we show our appreciation by teeming in hordes to backyard barbecues, riverbanks, towns, and best of all, your cities. So many donors! So little time until frost, although our Elite Squad may linger to delight you in December.

This year's Blood Drive will be held on Swamp Fest Day at Bogwater Lake. Mold and mildew will be posted to guide you to parking at Nailbed Plaza with shuttle service by Stragglers' Coach and Towing.

Again, this year, by request, we will be regaled by the maneuvers of The Massed Spider and Flea Drill Teams. Refreshments have been promised by O.D. Scumly and Sons Catering.

Be sure to wear short sleeves and short pants. Sandals are ideal for probing between toes. This year, we may surpass last year's quota. Thanks to R and D, more efficient extraction teams will be on hand and foot and elbow.

Looking forward to good needling and family fun,

Semper Sallow, Dir. Of PR

Flies

The Odium Boutique

Max Oder, Promotions Manager:

All that reeks and rots
My red eye kens,
Riches from the maggots' dens,
Enterprised by assiduous blowflies
In mating dances courtly, ritualized.

Laden in laces and scanty petticoats
How the shoppers sway their totes!
They bear fruits of dumpsters and carrion,
Orange peels and coffee grounds,
Egg shells and skeletons
Of creatures ripe for picking.
Feeding is the main desire.
I whet my legs in constant sawing
And probe in savory putrefaction.
A swashbuckler, I am velvet clad
With plumed hat (peacock feathers prized
From private pleasure gardens
Of Indian maharajahs),
And in the French manner,
Cavalier boots of motivation
To tread where man is loath to go.

Deeply I bow in salutation
And twirl my cuffs and ruff of Irish linen
With tatted edges gadrooned in Belgium.
A sight for rotting eyes am I
To bid you welcome to my shoppers' paradise.

Fleas

Jimmy Jump-Up, DJ:

Do the fleabag hop—
At Hotel Smarmy
The clerk is surly.
The air is murky.
Cast off your shoes
And inhibitions.
You'll uproot pillow cases
And smelly socks
Buried in blankets, unwashed,
That top infested mattresses.

Don't mind the lumps
Of uncoiled springs.
Don't bother to ring the bell;
No one's answering.
The view is gaudy neon blinking
Welcomes or warnings
Through worn window blinds.

If you linger, you'll be itching;
Red welts are maddening.
Check your pockets and coat linings.
Turn and spin; give a leap.
We'll nip those ankles
While you're cavorting.

The music's dreary; the view is bleak.
The light is flickering;
The carpet's gritty
And faucet drippy.
The smell is musty; the bureau's dusty;
Wallpaper's sagging, but don't be picky.
It's a room for the asking,
Whatever purposes you're sharing.

Bedbugs

Or L'amour De Nuit

Le Duc Du Sore:

Lascivious bedbugs—
At night when dreamers live private reveries,
We probe parts and leave bites of love
Caressed about their person.
In their mattresses or chairs
We prepare nests for l'amour.

Stealthy as stalker or lorn lover
We ride buses where new liaisons
Are always possible,
Where torn seat covers
Or seams are places where we dream.
We snuggle up pant legs
For a cuddle and leave a tickle
Followed by a red sprinkle.

In hotels of secret trysts,
We find new friends or victims
For tiny pincers' fleecing.
We marvel at their generosity of giving.
We bite and nip.
They are our paramours and playthings.

Leeches

Lance Capillaire, Recipient, Ivey Bleeder Award:

In tropical weederies
And river sludge,
Wrapped in roots, we trudge
Or ride on steamy tides
Where blooded bruisers go by,
And we fix our drinkers
On torso or thigh,
In nose or bum or rims of boots.

"Yum" is the word
That swims into mind
With dreams of red, incarnadine.
Non-clotting goo is the prize we share,
As humble needlers transmogrify
To tyrants of the blood.

When we've weakened our host
And bloated our most,
We coast from one to another,
A-float in murky water.
With loathsome quotas,
We count our conquests
In suckers, cozened and tapped,
And relax in the cozy afterglow
Of feeding or in bleeding donees.

Ants

Brother Emmet P.S. Mire:

Antlings, compose your legs. Stop combing your antennae and point them toward me. I speak to remind you that we have a proud heritage, and it is our duty to persevere in it. Indeed, we are the ultimate social conscience. We are selfless, so much so that we are drones in anonymous columns that live only to toil for the benefit of others. Our castes promote stability and efficiency.

We have no personal aspirations or desires and abhor calling attention to ourselves. That would be unpatriotic to the community. There is no room for individuality. Such striving is unseemly. It is so-o untidy, and worst of all, inefficient. We have shed that tyrant the self!

We are the very model of industrious organization. Men lag far behind us. They are busy competing and fighting among themselves. And so, it has fallen to us to be exemplars to humans though they are slow to learn, wayward, lazy, self-interested and self-righteous in their insistence to dominate all. Who can say they have been good for the planet? We do our best to clean up their messes.

Antlings, do not groan. We are up to the challenge! Remember there is no getting rid of us. You can rely on our motto: "Perseverance equals indestructibility."

Can you believe they blame us for ruining picnics? Can they not see that we express our gratitude and diligence by tidying the grass and carrying away the offerings they leave us? But, then, never trust the opinion of someone who cannot climb a table leg.

There may be hopeful signs from them. Their builders have learned from us. They are busy littering the landscape with giant anthills that we can admire and creep into along with other helpers they call "pests." So much food for us! So short a distance to crawl! They even pave trails to help other humans find their way home.

We, too, lay down trails as we tote the crumbs and stale food they leave for us. Our group conscience goads us to share our bounty with the colony. Do we object? Of course not! Service is the entire reason for our existence. We toil and always persevere. Humans should be so admirable and form columns of their own.

Antlings, do not become discouraged or confused. Let us pick up our banners and chant:

Speed is not needed

Altruism for all

Crusade

Re-commitment daily

I – the word to be shunned

Fun is work

Industriousness

Columns

Efficiency

Long may humans do homage to us and pay tribute with crumbs!

Worms

The High-Stepping Quartet From Anemia:
    Nema Todee
    Whip-Slinger
    Pin Spinner
    Lola The Looker With Her Hook

In the gullet
We raise havoc.
We purloin our provender
With Gastro our mascot.
Like felons we embezzle
Vitamins and minerals
From gullible intestines.
They spasm and twist
From such oppression.

For vulnerable victims,
We're vice-ridden
Vigilantes of victuals and viands.
Some call us parasites,
But others might say
We're enlightened to garner
Goodies from guts in perpetual night
Until the dread endoscope
Squirms into our palace,
And we are cast out, houseless, with malice
By various purges and remedies.

Meanwhile, in salute, use those extremities.
Let's kick up hook tails
And, like Lola, impale those entrails!

Spiders

Presented by: Leaperus,
Orator Laureate Arachneae

Alas, to be vilified before hatching,
To struggle from bondage breaking
Free to live 'though in shadows!
Oh, for the art and craft of web spinning,
Tenuous tendrils twined mystically in morning light
Then clumsily snapped by witless oafs.
This world is not safe for beauty.
How many legs must wipe tears for injustice?

Oh, for the dread of pursuers!
How many nestlings crushed by folded newspapers
Wielded by hands cruel and thoughtless!
Oh, for the reprieve of fastidious wrapping of pestilent
Prey in purest spun silk,
For wheeling eyes sharp on the hunt
And leaping limbs set on the target!

Our kind, the world abhors us.
Treacherous as we are deemed and doomed,
They snare us, spawned as they are from perfidy's nave
Yet declare themselves as ones who save
Though our destiny is made barren by their spiteful web!
Poisonous in plots and schemes they weave
Slanderous tales about us
And declaim their treason a boon.

Oh, for consolations of the vine, tippling fruit!
Gladitorially, we salute the resolute
And owners of multiple legs!

Rats

Mayor Felicitous:

Cadets, stop biting and sit up straight. Remember your dignity as heirs of the city.

We are crime lords of the streets. Strays run from us. Even humans fear us. The nasty stories you may have heard about us are true. We do not waste time on pleasantries or endearing ourselves to others. Remember: Surly is only a word. We have our turf to patrol and a city to colonize.

That shadow who turned a corner and disappeared likely was one of our cadets perfecting his technique for entrance into EAA (Executive Action Academy). When he graduates, you may see only his pellets, however excessive pelleting is a violation of EAA Charter, Article 28, "Our Responsibilities").

If we do not receive the required offerings from humans (See Article 17C, sub-section 31b of our EAA Charter,) we may chew tires overnight. Concrete is no obstacle. Humans strategically pour it so that we may hone our teeth by chewing it. They lay pipes underground and above for convenient runways for us. They pile their alleys with garbage and stuffed chairs as dorms and barricades and then complain we are taking control. Indeed, we are. Has no one noticed the city belongs to us? In time, resistance will crumble along with the city, and we still will be here.

Some of our kind have been kidnapped to run mazes (in violation of EAA Charter, Emergency Actions Committee "Resolution for Redress 142"). The outcome is always the same. We are smarter than humans expect, and we get mean when we are crowded. When will they learn?

There are dreadful rumors of horrors that are perpetrated in their labs, ghastly crimes beyond our imaginings or our desire to commit. However no one has escaped alive to confirm or deny these tales.

We have been villainized for bearing diseases, although some might say we do nature's work of limiting population (Humans reproduce like rabbits) while we make room for our kind. Is that mean? We could ask: Are humans to be relied on for kindness? Some might call it a rat-eat-rat world, but, I ask you, to which rats do they refer?

And so, cadets, as you go forth to establish your turf, be wary. Devious minds have devised fiendish schemes and treacherous traps that await you.

Locusts

Draco, Lead Navigator:

Being swarm-ish
Does not make us smarm-ish.
Actually, we are clean and dry,
And some like us fried.

Rubbing legs can be a whir, a trill, a thrill
When we congregate, then mate
And populate fields with progeny.
Pestilence is an unkind word
For our togetherness.
Sharing is a nicer thought.

True, we travel in herds
That fill the sky like birds
Whose wings are myriad
And appetite deleterious.

Farmers abhor us,
But I think of us as gypsies
Seeking our reward
As we scour plain and field
For sustenance.

Nowhere do we find
Welcome on our weary way. And why?
It is a conundrum to share
When each claims all that is there.
Stripping is what we do to grain,
Thus, we are blamed
As a rabble who scrabble to survive,
Yet of reapers we might say the same.

Squirrels

Grumple Tailskins,
Recruiter, Forestry Studies, Passivity U.

There are no stars named for us,
No constellations, though we abound
Between earth and sky,
To celebrate our perseverance or trickery,
Our single-focused search for acorns
Or service to the forests.

What we bury and then forget
Begets a leafy legacy,
A crowned monarchy of mammoth trees
Beyond our paw-span stewardry.
We build our nests in swaying canopies,
Comb and stroke our expressive tails,
The only cause of vanity.

We pursue larger themes of daring and agility
And bury what we love
For future transcendency.
No one mourns our dashing duels with cars
Or notes the wit of threading steps on overhead wires.
We are blamed for fires
Though sacrificed to electric chews.

We, who race up and down tallest trees
And leap from limb to limb as if winged,
Are not baffled by feeders of mere human ingenuity.
Our deeds of speed in tree heights have seethed
Our brains, astrally
And ignited frippery or myths
Of the bird-seed Viking
Who has pillaged every feeder
And dared the mighty hawk
With a glare of rightful tenancy.

Lordlings that we are and knights errant
In the cause of trees that reach to the heavens,
There are no stars named for us.

Yellowjackets

Leo Zinger:

We make our nests in humble earth
Where there's a dearth
Of tasty savories.
We gravitate on flitting wings
To garbage cans of viands.

We dress in stripes
Where trash is ripe for sifting
And prioritize barbecues and picnics.
We land on hands that clutch hot dogs or buns
And swarm on ears of corn streaming butter.
We rush to nosh, nibble and sample
Where burgers and slaw,
Salads and wings are ample.
Over melons and pies or salty fries
We hover, as it were, relishing.

Ants, our neighbors, may think us rash
To feast on trash,
But we are humble
To rummage in tonnage of garbage.
Our queens and larvae are hungry.

In all this plenitude,
We can get testy
And let loose some stingers,
If humans get greedy and nasty
And refuse to share their scandalous bounty.

Moth

Cosmo Linter,
Lead Hole Maker

In the garden I am a pretty sprite,
My wings gaily fluttering
In a dance upon currents of air,
Wafting from leaf to leaf,
Yet a sad sight when lured to lights
That singe my wings
'Though gladly I turn to dust.
Humans might learn from me
To embrace eventuality.

Refrain:
Housebound I creep from one nocturnal dreaming
On woolen sweaters to coats feasting.
Settled I am for a long winter's keeping
In precious abode for my young.

How fortunate for humans
That I urge them to new trends,
So much fresher than old garments mended!

For kindly sheep I am a boon.
Busily they keep rampant grass tended
By assiduous grazing and chewing,
Their work always needed, never ending
In making miraculous wool
To replace all my gnawing ruins.

Where would shepherds and their clever dogs be without me?
Or the yarn spinners, the knitters, the darners, the weavers,
The giant mills humming, the tailors, the sellers
Of clothing and blankets?

Why does no one thank me
For the jobs my chewing engenders?
For untiring service to the economy?

What thoughtless, small-minded ingratitude!

Section Four

Silly Poems

Dog

Where the dogwood, dog rose and dogtooth violet grow
Roads may dogleg. There are dog days and sun dogs
And moon dogs in one or two-dog nights
When the dog star shines while we work the dogwatch.
War aces hold dogfights in the sky. Seadogs ride the tides.
Winners are lucky dogs, but some men are dogs
Or dirty dogs or sly old dogs who offend with dog-breath
Or call misfavored women "dogs."
Someone may be a top dog, a hound dog, a mutt or a cur.

We distrust puppy love and bark up the wrong tree
Or lie down with dogs and get fleas.
We dogpaddle, fleaflicker, dogtrot or hotdog it
And bark our shins or howl that our dogs hurt.
We scrape dog-doo off our shoes
Or misspeak and step in it. We bark orders,
Growl, snarl and show our canines like junkyard dogs
Or sleep in the doghouse when we are dog-tired in a dog's life
In a dog-eat-dog world where we have a dog's chance.
Dogfaces wear dog-tags and clerics wear dog collars.
We shop in flea markets, but dog ticks may bite,
And people may get sick as dogs with hangdog faces.
We would not wish it on a dog or feed dogsbody to a dog,
Though doggie bags follow diners home, like lost puppies.
We catch dogfish, eat corndogs, hushpuppies and dogs on buns
Or throw someone a bone to gnaw on his problems
When the tail wags the dog, though we let sleeping ones lie.

We hire dog catchers.
Some of us howl at the moon.
We root for the underdog or dog-knap,
Or hound someone, nip at his heels or dog his trail.
We persist in dogged determination, read dog-eared pages,
Write doggerel, weave houndstooth, drive dogsleds
And sleep in pup tents or fleabags but hope everyone has his day
Though it may rain _____ and dogs,
Dog gone it.

Tantara

(This word-game poem includes names
of numerous musical instruments.
I count 60. How many can you find?)

"Tantara! Tantara!," the blast of trumpet
Screams, "I am and am and am."
Tan snares the tambourine.
Tara thwiddles harp-C-chord-i-an.
Congas pound a shawm.
Uke and bugle horn the flugel.
Glacken spiels a tune.
"O-carina!" sighs bassoon,
And carillon chimes tune.
Tin whistle tears tinsel.
A-jimble plinks the spoons.
Kettle clinks a cymbal.
Marimba plucks a piccolo.
Skeley-bones jumps a-jiggle.
Pipes moan in frantic fringle.
Harmonica gets nausea.
Harmonium gets cranked.

Who-is-masked hones the axe.
The sax groans a-tone-meant.
The tenor's alto far.
Elbow bumps the cello.
Oboe blows a nose.
Ulna thumbles tabla.
Timbrel beats triangle.
Piano duels a moog.
Tubas sneeze kazoo.
Femur flips French horn,
And bass is lost and lorn.
A-tremble whines the viol.

Finger-bones-a-wiggle frets the fiddle.
Guitar pluncks a zither.
Dulcimer flicks feather.
Banjo frales and rales.
Man-done-in strums mandolin.

Gorgon rips the organ.
Cornet torments a hornet.
Fife and tabor wake the neighbors.
Clavier gets rav-i-er.
Hoot-it-up plays fast,
And loose has the juice.
Tooter jupes a flute.
Dobro does do-se-do.
Didger honks i-doo.
Maracas knock and mock.
Clarinet cracks dishes,
And castanet lures fishes.
Clappers get giddier.
Xylophone gets whacked.
Drum dinks pitty-tat.
Trombone-y zoots a-tone-y.
Sitar ragas Zanzibar.
Tantara, Tantara!

Our Heroes Rode Horses

Our heroes rode horses,
Roy on Trigger, Dale on Buttermilk,
Gene on Champion, Hopalong on Topper,
The Lone Ranger on Silver, Tonto on Scout.
We trusted them in time of trouble.
They taught us good guys win in the end
And to be straight shooters,
To tell the truth, mind our teachers
And our manners, pick up our toys
And put our cap guns in our holsters.

We learned that bad white men speak
With forked tongue
And hide their mouths behind bandannas.
We were taught not to ride our horses hard
Because they are the friends of our imaginations
And would save us, keep us ready to escape from outlaws.
Noble Silver, Scout, golden Trigger, Buttermilk
Champion and Topper flew us over prairies and canyons
And hid us from drygulchers and bushwhackers.

Lash on Black Diamond showed us bullwhips,
Triumphed over gunslingers.
Cisco showed us silver conchos on tight pants,
Charming manners, a big hat and rode Diablo
Through our dreams.   Pancho on Loco proved a true friend.
Masked Zorro on black Toronado could hide
Within a cape, and showed lithe grace of an aerialist
To scale flowered balconies
And righted wrongs with sword-slashed Z's.

Matt Dillon on Buck loved Miss Kitty
Chastely and non-judgmentally.
Doc Adams was shrewd, and Chester limped.
Squint-eyed Festus rode his john-mule Ruth.
He quivered his eye menacingly.
Was this when he recalled the Confederacy?

Wild Bill Hickok on Buckshot hurtled over plains.
Mustachioed Paladin on Rafter embodied chivalry,
Clad in black, ever ready to rescue ladies
Or haul bad men off to jail, hogtied across their pommels.
He proffered White Knight cards to seekers
In palmy hotel courts of San Francisco.

Faithful sidekicks were the allies we needed,
Though Andy sagged, a doughy pillow, on Joker,
And Smiley trooped on Ring Eye.
Pat Brady chugged on four-wheeled Nellie Belle,
And Gabby was cranky on Eddie, Calico or Blossom.
Ladies were always answered, "Maam,"
And men were, "sir."
Young buckeroos brushed their ponies
And mucked their stalls dutifully,
Without being told.

Now that we are quaint
With our straight-shooter values,
Who will tie our horses to the hitching rail?
Who will be our "pardners" in adventures?

Birds Stage A Play

Deacon Crow directs the show.
Magpie struts and steals
A scene from Madame Drillwood.
The Noble Duke of Jayblue rants and scrapes
His whine down the spine.
'Rascible Red, the Cardinal, keeps the time.
Mrs. Downy-Peck corrects the script.
Harrier is the editor.
Nuthatch controls the curtains.
Pelican strains his lines and cries,
"How I try! How I try!
Ducklings dodge their cue.
Dove laments the review.

Herr Grosbeak chatters his aside off stage right.
Chickadee cries, "Oh me, oh my!
How Lady Robin lingers!"
Starling steals the stage light.
Little Wren is in the play pen.
Woodthrush rushes the scene.
Sparrow spares no digging for the meaning,
The motivation for emoting.
Who-Who has chewed the painted trees
And frighted Prop-Master Mouse to hiding?

Dame Specklebreast fires her agent
And will not appear without representation.
Sir Hawksbeak culls the no-talent seekers.
Bob-O-Link guards the stage door.
Finches spray the stage with millet.
What more could Owlet do to guide the few
To proper enunciation?
Grouse powders his wig in indignation.
Grackle contemplates a tragedy
For his next production.

Junco trundles tubs of tickets.
Flicker settles the bickering for a theme.
Titmouse wears a top hat
And poses for his picture.
Cockatoo raises his crest for top billing.
He fusses, "Who-Who has smeared my mirror
With greasepaint?"
Egret refuses to donate plumes
And sells tickets to the Herons
Who clamor for fish fingers at intermission.
Ptarmigan is off again.
Penguin rents a tux.

Colonel Peacock provides inspiration.
Bluebirds croon a chorus.
Miss Byrd-Hum flits at will
And does not tend the till.
Turkey trills and wobbles.
Garrulous Gulls distract the audience.
Flamingos insist on a water pool
In the orchestra pit.
They fume in pink consternation.
Geese heckle and hiss at rehearsals.
Condor circles overhead.

Private Rail peers through the sedge
At Curvy Curlew
Who calls for a curfew.
Shrike calls for a strike for scale wages.
Canvasback takes a survey.
Kookaburra whirrs and wheedles.
Hoopoe checks the lease for loopholes.
Pigeon revels in indecision.
Bunting goes indigo.
B. Eater searches for a hive.

Harpy keeps on target
With Secretary's notes.
Peewit plans her comeback
In Roadrunner's tour.
Redshank calls for more.
Who-Who calls critics "snakes?"
Crake and Coot lure Big-wing Buzz Ard
Into backing S. and Piper.
Rook and Mari Bou do soft shoe
On Stage left.

Eagle swoops and glides
Peregrine gyrates in the skies.
Captain Crane whoops wildly,
And Cassowary hides.
Meadowlark goes on a caper.
Countess Emu races Diva Rhea.
Corporal Stork watches from a chimney
And declares a tie.
Miss Oriole takes tickets
And coaxes Lady Bugs from thickets.
Mr. Bower hunts trinkets.
Parakeets swing on vines.
Mynah recites her lines.

Partridge and Canary cry, "How very ordinary!
Our talents require better scripts!"
Whippoorwill weeps for melodrama.
Senor Birdo-Paradiso craves romance.
Peahens press for temperance.
Lorikeets and Ravens want raisins.
Ovenbird bakes a seed pie.
Quail retreats beneath a pail.
Pheasant is effervescent.
Thornbirds are feeling brittle.
Cowbirds jangle bells and clatter cymbals.
Mockingbird whistles a tune,
And loon plays the spoons.
Who – Who can pound a drum?

"Cheap! Cheap!" cries the costumer,
"What am I to do without enough fluff?"
Eider replies, "It is either you or I!"
Teal has drowned the film reel.
Parrot preens for the camera.
Macaw demands a monologue.
Lovebirds are self-involved and late.
Swans will not negotiate.
Tanager claims stage manager.
The producer prefers the absurd.
Warblers prefer abstraction.

The albatross is at a loss.
Goonies and Boobies swoop for a nautical theme.
The Auks gawk and squawk.
The Ernes and Terns need a shoreline view.
Nightingale wants a moonlit setting
Osprey refuses the invitation.
Kites want bright light and wind.
Sapsucker prefers litigation.
Swallows want mitigation.
Vulture settles in the rafters and tends the exits.
Madame Hen cries, "Cluckers! Cluckers all!
Grit is in my gullet!

Magnus, The Pug

Magnus the Pug
Reads every fireplug
In the neighborhood.
His intense sniffing
And questions
Lead to more snuffling
To clue out answers,
But telltale odors
And more nosing
From different angles
Turn up tales
Of love triangles
And jealousies
Over willing ladies
Or assessments
Of suitors' necessities.

There are quarrels,
Long settled,
Still posted on lampposts
Or cautions to the unwary
About intruding
On someone else's sanctuary.
Magnus sometimes scratches
Earth and kicks it,
Dismissively, behind him.
Snorting is a warning
Of his supremacy
In his patch of dogdom.
Tail chewers or pink collars
Are *non grata* in these strata
Unless worn by misses
Accompanied by governesses.

Magnus courts the red bandana look.
Lavender is for sissies.
He prefers a spiky collar
With bike-chain pendant.
A leggy Dane
Lives in his dreams
Of her stately carriage
And fulsome thighs.
His heart sighs
With every twitch
Of her nordic whiskers.
He consoles himself
With steak bones and scraps of fat
And peach ice cream
Or a rummage in the garbage,
But naught can satisfy his longing.

Other ladies have assets to offer.
The gypsy mongrel
With the knowing strut
Stirs his thrust
For wanderlust.
He thinks it unkind
To call her a 'mutt'
For lack of proper breeding.
He eyes her self-reliant gait,
But his heart is pinned
On dreams of his nordic diamond,
Though her nose and his can never meet,
And a tender lick evades him.
Her eyes, upraised through lashes thick
Are far above his stature.
How can his lovelorn gaze attract her?

Alas for loves
That never know fulfillment,
For the pining of heart's lament
Or the vagaries of fate!
Lengthy devotion may not win
The prize,
But it may lead to ennoblement.
Magnus' lesson is learned
That as love is not bound
By stature,
Neither is it earned.

Dullis Dishwater

Dullis Dishwater
Goes to the store
For groceries and gasoline,
Muffled in scarf, coat and cap,
Anonymous,
While at home,
The laundry soaks,
And dishcloths are in order.
Scrubbed floor, wet mop drying,
Curlers tightening against her scalp
Prove she is a dutiful drone.

She used to hope for more,
But since he is a bore,
She watches soaps
Where lives of fiction
Have more scope
And are the most
Relief she can hope.
With chips and dips
Or chocolates
She consoles and drugs
Some remnant of her girlhood self
Who thought that life had more
Promise for Dullis.

She fancies romance,
A handsome hero,
A fashion runway
Or stage door
Where adorers wait with bouquets,
Or she suns on crystal beaches
Sipping a drink with umbrella,
An orchid tucked behind her ear.

She wonders, "Is it wrong
To long for more
Or simply futile?"
Did I forgo some happy chance
To stay with the usual chores
And iron his pants?

Too Small

It's too small to be a dog.
It came home like a black-eyed
Baked potato, sprouting tufts of hair.
It barks and sniffs, scratches,
Licks impolite spots, burps and passes gas.
Mercifully, it goes outdoors
And spares the orientals.
It trots and smells like old socks
And gets fleas if unattended.
Dry mess clings to its banner tail.
It turns a bath to wrestling contest;
The winner is the one less wet.

No lap can sit unadorned
From its hairy presence.
My book perches on its head
As it circles to find a spot to curl.
Flop-eared, its claws click and clatter
On wood floors, distractingly
In my morning resistance to waking.
It pants in my nose
And claws the new mattress,
Demanding I play with Squeaky or Ducky.

It's underfoot and over loud,
Goes snarling, snag toothed psychotic
On meeting a bewildered Saint Bernard,
But it squats and leaks submissively
At the feet of every new person it meets.
It yelps and challenges
The nasty, big, black dog next door
Whose deep bark reverberates
Menacingly through a shaky wood fence.
They both charge, and I must wade
In mud to reclaim it.

It rarely comes when called
And hides and whines in storms,
Never gets enough to eat,
Paws in birdseed on the deck,
Tracks it through the house,
Claws deep grooves in my back door
And pre-warns the squirrels it chases
With its shrieking.
It flies two inches above the ground
And leaps too high for safety,
But it's too small to be a dog.

Fish Jamboree*

Pilot leads the way.
Flagfish waves a pennant.
Hake and Manta Ray,
Clown and Grouper
Congregate to celebrate
An underwater year
Of nets evaded, hooks, harpoons
And spears eluded
And bait not taken.

Hammerhead and Sawfish build a stage.
Lantern lights it for the players
While Sunfish beams on Shad.
Tilefish lays the floor.
Sailfish makes a curtain.
Right Whale wires for sound.
Electric Eel embraces a make-up mirror.
Roughy sets up props and paints them orange.
Flounder takes soundings.
Skate runs errands,
While urchins scour the floor,
Pointed Pike and Marlin proclaim the news
And put on their tap shoes,
Sea Cows jangle neck bells,
But Yellowbelly feels faint at the thought
Of taking part.
Fathead claims the director's chair.

Orca conducts the orchestra.
Porpoises form a chorus.
Angler waves his lure
At Rainbow dancers' high kicks,
And Seals clap time.
Seahorse reins in eely slide tromboners.

Turtle thumps a drum.
Remora trips across the organ stops.
Bluefish flute while Angel plucks the harp,
And Blowfish plays Darters.
Guppies thrum the corals.
Tuna toots a tuba.
Pickerel plays piccolo.
Shark strums guitar.
Jellies play the cello.
Maned Lionfish bows the violin.
Foureye Butterfly does magic tricks.
And Bass bassoons.
Leatherjacket rides a motorcycle.
Mackerel plays marimba.
Parrots chortle with Seahorses.
Koi curtsy coyly
Lampreys can-can clad in pantalets
As they do pirouettes.
Stripers slide into a dance
While Arrowtooth grins reassuringly.
Sperm Whales hum, and Trumpetfish blares a horn.
The Bermuda crew tings triangles.
Betas intone the alphabet.
Bullhead refuses to learn his lines.
Sardines key the concertina,
And Conger beats the bongos.

Shrimp craves big scenes.
Sole wants the lead role,
But Starfish steals the show.
Abalone weeps to be alone.
Lemon Shark has lost her powder puff.
Minnow plays queen for a day.
Menhaden trades beads with Moray
Who calls on Perch to search for more with Dragonet..
Humpbacks clump together.
Cod and Scrod form a pod.
Oyster lies abed.

Clams shovel sand.
Cuttlefish nestles with the Seals,
Gnomefish chases Goblin Shark
While Dogfish howls at Sicklefin Hound.
Swordfish fences with Grenadier.
Sturgeon wants to be a surgeon..

Octopus inks a contract with caterers.
Coelacanth seals cans.
Warty Orandas tat doilies.
Nettles put the kettle on.
Squid opens a lid for Sea Cucumbers.
Mako makes cupcakes.
Sea Snakes ice teacakes.
Sponge trades recipes with Smooth-Tongue.
Alewife serves drinks,
And Clownfish tends the bar
Where Lizardfish lounges with the Gar.
Hogfish guards the banquet table.
Anemones lack energy.
Weakfish lifts weights.
Snails set the place cards.
Sockeyes polish silver,
And Wrasse washes dishes.
Trout lets Boxfish out.
Carp and Blenny complain loudly.
Herring are averse to sharing,
And Monk abstains.

The noisy celebrations
Keep Clams up late.
Oysters spit pearls in irritation.
While Conchs swing their partners
And undulate.
Sandfish and kelp
Swirl around the Garden Eels.
Lobsters and Crabs shake castanets
With their claws.

Corals turn red in indignation.
Amid the raucous hoedown,
Hermits tap their shells on Turbots
And leave tracks in the sand,
While all hope next year
Brings them together again
For another Jamboree.

*How many sea creatures can you count? I count 118.

A Rheumy Numeral Lettered Sailor

(This poem is a word game and a love story. Roman
numerals that are capitalized, and letters from the Greek
alphabet are used to replace sounds of syllables or words.)

A bowlegged sailor with tattoos
Of a Mermaid, an anchor and sloop
Awoke from a floundering snooze
And D-*psi*-red to take a Cruise.
He thought to forecastle
On going smokeless
And learning to wear a shoe
His sole to enlarge, himself to Improve
For his porpoise of winning
Miss L-C, his Lady Love
Who subsisted on *Mu*-ssels and Cod
But never Clammed haddock or scrod.
'Though she smelt of Lilies and gillyflowers,
Her eyes held the blue
Of Tahitian skies,
And her Cheeks wore the pink
Of Papeete sunrise.

Angel fish harped
Her Carp-ish red Lips,
The gold of her koi Complexion
And the swell of her furled Marquesas.
They Chantey-ed In praise
Of her Manta rays and the kelp-ish sway
Of her hips as her parasol Dipped,
And she caravelle-D Like gazelle
Springing and Chewing
On Malabar Candy.
Sashaying in shade
Of ships in the port,

Her aft sail gave joy to the Lads on board
Who whistled and hooted, "Sulawesi!"

She ambled the strand
And Disported herself grandly
On the hand of a Spanish grandee
Whose Mustachios flowed over his nose,
Though his goatee grew quite slowly.

Gold flecks shone In his Coat
And silver threads on his head.
His rapier rattled in scabbard
O'er his toes when he waddled with L-C.
On the head of his walking stick, twisted,
A dragon Leered Most fiercely.
Grandee implored, "Leave the fleet on the shore
To the care of others less handy!
Be my Lily, My rose,
I'LL polish your toes!
You'LL be My Conquistador
If you abandon the shore
And the Lads you adore
And galleon my stallion
Who waits at your Door!"

On seeing her wavering
'Tween youth and the graying
Grandee sniffled and piffled
While his earring shriveled,
"Alas, My Lass, the hourglass trickles,
And sand flows with the tide.
It's you will Make a bonny bride,
And It's I will be at your side
With My gold at the ready!
When there's a quickening In your belly
Will you choose My doubloons
Or baboons from the fleet at the shore?"

When told of the plan, Mother yawl-ed
And ketch-ed her breath.
She cried, "Oh, Madeira! What Cordoba story is this?
And what will your otter say?
You topsail his Life!
What gain will this strife nettle him?
What will it alameda him?
His blood pressure is high,
And his temper is low!
I fear that this selfish
Blowfish will send him awry
To Caraway Bay and Point Desperation!
And what will the neighbors say?"

With sinking tattoos sailor rued the news.
He *psi*-ed and *xi*-ed and Cried, "Aruba!
I'LL *eta* swordfishier Sandwich
And garnish It with Pitcairn-ish dip
Myself to Console and feel Less alone-i-er.
It'LL Cure My pickle In brine!"

He spied a fleet of X-L-ent ships
Whose admiral ordered fish and chips.
"I, I, sir!" was the reply.
"M-M," the Sir said, "I!"
"Look, Look! C, C!" the Lookout foretold.
"I C M, I C M!" the gob espied,
"But where's their Cannon?
Where's their powder?
Phi, phi, a *pi*-rate's flag I behold!
And who will turn M to Chowder?"

In a roar heard on shore
The admiral swore, *"Epsilon!*
I'D sprit My jib
Ere I'D shark My Duty
Or see My ships or Crew
Be *pi*-rate's booty!

I'D be squid if I Did
Let the octo-
Push My brass buttons
 Or unnerve My reserve!
I'D rip My epaulets in a fit
And be stripped aft of My brass, for sure!"

Then the admiral raged at the na-V,
"D-stroy their D-ployers!
D-molish their topdeck!
D-spair periscope!
Overwhelm the helm!
Smoke their stacks
And Crack their hatches!
Mangle their Mainsail!
Batten their capstans
And splinter their Mizzen!
Unravel their pulleys
And set moths on their wooly suits!"

And so the admiral thundered,
"Scope that float
And parge that barge!
Tote the buckets that cause a ruckus!
Scupper their rudders
And scuttle their gunnels!
Pillage their bilge!
A-beam their bream!
Ahoy the oyster with unseemly roister!
Scrape the keel
And peel that tin Can!
Deep six the Davits!
Winch their pumps!
Dump the Cargo on Davy's Locker
And barnacle his britches!
Man the dinghy!
Oar that thing-y!
Do In the flotilla!

Leave not one scintilla
Or *iota* afloat
On the C-C foam!

Thus the sailor Despaired
Of braiding red herring
Or winning the Lovely Miss L-C.
He glugged some grog,
Jamaica rum and ale
Then exhaled and breathed Deeply
The salty C air
That Cleared runnel eyes and the frog in his throat.
He whistled a jig and Danced a hornpipe
And tied a Love knot
Of coarsest Manila hemp-en.
He tossed his *kuppa* to fishes
Along with his wishes
Of wooing Miss L-C, the fair.
Then he scrimshawed the tooth
Of a whale.

Shanghai-ed in Peru,
He joined a *chi*-rew
Hunting Marauding Marlins
And skulking the wily tarpon.

They Indulged in a *gamma*
To *rho* the dice of polar ice
Loaded with Capers and Coral.
He cried, "*Omicron*, Life
Has *delta* bad hand!
I'LL Cleave to My *alpha* Cat
Who Likes to gnaw sprat
And I'LL *omega* bowl
Of *nu lambda* stew!"
He *mu*-sed on Losses
Of *pi-nu*-pple tarts
And brooded on *tau*-Dry
Wounds to his heart.

In udder frustration
He Cried to goats that gamboled on board,
"You Ma-a-h at Me blandly
Which angers Me Madly!
I'LL bow to return to the stern
When anchors aweigh
And belay Chatter-some
Parakeets In the sheets
Or the Monkeys a-stealing My grub.
Then I'LL sip on a Mandalay tokay!"

The crew sailed *upsilon* to eastern seas
For Crates of *pi*-payas and Ceylon tea
And braved Many a tropical storm.
They *beta tau* paycheck
Of finding riches
Avast the wide *Sigma Zeta*.
Then Lost in a Muddle
They went searching for Mangoes
And Mired boat In the Mangroves
And Carelessly *kappa-psi*-zed.
They waded ashore
On palmy beaches
Then ran from Cannibals and Leeches.
They wove rattan hats and dined on bats
They snared by their screeches.

Past C-gulls a-screaming
And Circling ernes
They sailed along shorelines
Of roaring sea lions
And walruses preening In Mud
Who Lifted their whiskers
And shook Ivory tusks
At orcas sporting a tux.
A frolicsome Mollusk
Went chasing a scallop
On the trail of a breaching blue whale.

Penguins trundled to nests In the sand
While Manatees koi-ly sheening in shallows
Lumbered past turtles
Engirdled in C-weed
And Dreaming of krill.
A sturgeon went Lurching In search of a perch
To fill his entrails with Lunch.
Otters went Mobbing,
Star anemones hobbling.
Damsel fish In Distress
Fled from a gar-ish *pike*
While eels wove a shield,
And triggerfish fired an attack.
Lobsters Menaced with CLaws,
And Crabs Crepe-D aside,
While C-horses Chortled In foam.
In all the disturbance some plankton got Cranky
And reddened the tide In their Ire.
A Lost albatross ducked Loons and a tern
On a Mission to pluck parrots
That gnawed on their pennant
And perched on the Mizzen.

The whole *alpha chi*-rew
In throes of a fever
Spied a thatched Cottage
Where steaming pottage
Appeared In a Vision Mirage-IC.
They Casaba-ed for home
And abalone wept Lone
In their Longing for grouper.

When at Last sailor returned
Miss L-C then Learned

Of his pearl-Less adventures.
He furled to his knees
And uttered his pleas
To sail In her Current of Love.
She tipped back her plumed hat
And flowing Long tresses
While Counting her ten-button gloves
And regarded his shabby attire.
She told of her true Love
For fancy dresses
Thusly spurned his advances
And said, "I have Learned
That riches are better than wishes,
And Lilies smelt better than fishes."

Sailor blubbered and Cried,
"It's just Molucca!
I'D walk a plank
For the touch of those flanks
And thighs like a rising gannet!
What hope have I
When I'Ve Lost to a Lubber
The fairest Menhaden
Ever Isle-D by Man?
Her sequins and spangles
And red hair that Dangles
To the grace of her waist
Have enflamed Me to Madness
And harpooned My poor heart
And held It In tow
To the harbor of Hades!
She Cast Me In torment
And kept Me In foment
Up to this Moment!"

So, sorely Disparaged
He hoved to a Carriage
And shouted, I'M off to C

Where a Man Can be free
To sail the wide *Sigma Zeta!*
Alone, I'M a prize In somebody's eyes!
I'LL trawl Islands of beauty
Where welcoming Ladies

Will C My true worth!
You can bet your pelican
There's a Lady who'LL say,
To halibut! I'll have M!
Though there's tar on his hands
And grease on his spanner,
I could Learn to Love him In troth
'Cause he's a treasure-some turbot!"

Gallantly flourishing rattan hat
And smelling of sprat,
Sailor bowed Like a brig
That ploughs rough troughs
In a swirling ocean.
Splitting his britches,
He tugged up his hitches
And blew farewell kisses
To Miss L-C at Last.

When his back turned away,
Her heart burned
And Murmured a warning.
Though she rued her Choice,
She held the InVoice
For her Latest purchase
Of Lemur and petticoat,
A VerVet and stockings of silk.
Fine Laces braced her resolve
And Comforted her wallet
Of tapestried swans.

In this tale there's a MoraL
Of Lovers parted by greed:
Both riches and sorrow
In Measure unequal
Return to the salty C.

Section Five

Poems

The Country Is My Heart

The country is my heart,
Its hills my heights,
Valleys shelters of repose,
Its inland seas, memory.
Rains and snows nourish my growth.

In deep forests of fallen leaves
I am a searcher on lost paths
That meet in meadows of light.
My ancient trees hold histories
Of times past and engender those to come.

New trees spring from ashes,
Praise the triumph of green.
The deer roam my glades
And vanish in shadows
To re-appear with dappled flanks.

Waterfalls are my loves
And jagged rocks my sorrows.
Ferns overgrow my losses.
Moss wraps about my patience
And makes it whole.

I flow in songs of water over stones.
Currents braid the sands
In trails of passing.
I swim with finned ones
And shimmer in light-filled streams.

I fly with eagles or mourn with doves.
Birds speak my languages
Of love and seeking.
They grace my skies
In arcs of wings weaving.

Tall grasses sway in heartbeats
Of my unbounded plains.
They yearn toward the sky
Where the wind reveals paths
Of the spirit's flight.

My deserts are dry seasons of sustenance
Where small lives thrive.
I am mountains that rise
In spines of my endurance and rebirth
Freed from the cover of clouds.

Mermaid On My Kitchen Wall

The mermaid sails on my kitchen wall,
Slim waisted, firm flanked, up-breasted
With fulsome tail noiselessly
Parting paper waves.
Her hair, a mantle or sail, splayed
In echoes of tropic wind
Rustles painted fronds of palm.
Her arm carelessly trails
In the curl of her spell.
Her left arm beckons me to join
Or waves farewell.

Someone crafted her scales of tin,
The metallic, cyan sheen of skin.
Her ageless figure, youth itself,
Is not misshapen by decades
As with a mortal frame.

Some oceanic longing overtakes me,
A keening message sunken
In my conch shell ear,
A whisper of far-flung currents
The soul navigates,
And I yearn to greet her in the whitecaps,
Dazzled by the sun's dance,
In play with the dolphins.

The springtime ribbon I have bound
About her hanging chain
Gaily prevaricates in the stilled, stale air of my wall
Where she flies unchained in liquid soul
And wields her mirror.
Timeless maiden, unassailable
In the currents of deeper being
Reflects a restoring self.

She flies from me
Or seeks to set me free,
But the brand of mortality,
Hissing in coils
Upon my spirit, sears
And would quench it,
'Though I tread the currents' chop
And bob without her in the deep.

Sail on, maiden,
Beyond the reach of chains or walls,
Beyond mortal tides or brands
When youth seems oceanic,
All embracing, everlasting.
Sail on beyond the hourglass shore
Where gulls clamor and tides roar,
Where mortals wave and crave to bathe
In the currents that you master.
Sail on to the steady deeps
Where the spirit aches and seeks relief.

Lake

Wind whiffs across the water
In sighing laps mildly, indulgently
Welcoming an embrace,
Breathing souls enlaced.

A lone swan,
Entranced upon a rippling mirror,
Watches for a returning mate,
Scans the skies,
In summer fullness minds
The hum of dragonflies
Whose wings vibrate tensely.
He lingers as brown leaves moulder,
Sunken regretfully,
When ice clutches his feathers,
And pale flakes distress the surface
As if ashes had tears
For fallen wings.

Camille

I.
The painter's beloved
Sits cramped in a boat small, walled.
She is isolated, a dark figure, face unshown,
Bent as in pain, clutching her abdomen
Or reading, perhaps a book,
Perhaps an omen, sorrowing.
The boat's enclosing walls are stark
Against the river's melting greys
As the sky lours on a clouded day.
The boat's reflection, flowing,
Serves to blend as one the boat,
The beloved and the river's end
Amid encircling trees
Of grey and ashen green leaves.

II.
There is no place
For the beloved to go.
Her passing seems foreknown
In the painter's vision.
The boat is a pale apparition
And she a wisp of darkness,
An islet afloat, unmoored,
A steepened cloud or stain
Caught in the river's passing,
And yet that sorrow and apprehension
Linger in beholders' hearts afresh,
Borne from the past into the future,
Made current by the painter's brush
And solaced by the artist's touch.

Fall Reservoir

There is a deep holding in the reservoir,
A silence of hearts, compressed,
A darkness in depths, pent,
Where beings have met formal endings.
Towns are drowned, road signs in place,
Roofs and shutters oddly forlorn
In a gloom where fishes roam.

Man-built walls hold flooded farms
Patiently worked, the sweat of horses,
Lathered, in the plowman's harrowing,
Who clawed that earth for sustenance.
Now drowned are the core of orchards
And winding presses, the sap of trees
That sweetened hard-wrested meals.

Unrecalled are secrets of lives worn
In toil, spent, who have mourned
War dead and those lost young,
As the earth has bedded bones,
Hopes and losses of the heart,

And on the surface, a calm riffling moves
On greyness in currents shallow,
Changeable, malleable to the wind
In a fullness as of dreaming
On shoals stray swans have graced.

In ragged vee's over-winging, pilgrim geese
Find consolation, settle, breed.
In last refuge, displaced deer and furtive fox
Steal among shadows and laurels.
In dull light the husk of winter withers.
On hillsides, pall-bearer pines
Loom in a requiem for brighter times.

Feeble, haunted, car lights creep
Across a bridge over lost years.
Soon the night obscures shores
And stands of oak and hickory.
Clouds flee a sinking moon.
There is a silence, a weight bearing
An abyss that consumes.

Robert

Robert haunted my childhood. This is not to say that he asked to crowd me with tales of the artist and war hero I could never be. No, my mother made certain his memory would survive as long as I live. She would haul out her treasured scrapbook of newspaper clippings of his deeds and drawings and tell me that Robert, her older brother, was the person she loved most in this world.

In his B-17 Flying Fortress he shot down the first plane at which he aimed in his very first raid over enemy territory. His position as right waist gunner in the cumbersome design made it unlikely to hit anything, but Robert had an artist's eye and hand coordination. In one article, the pilot praised Robert as the reason for the success of their mission, but in his last letter home, Robert revealed that he "hated raining down death on women and children."

The newspapers had dubbed him "the flying artist of the air." The "boys," as they were called, were not allowed to take photos of their loved ones up in the planes with them lest they fall into enemy hands, but they were permitted to take the drawings Robert had assiduously made of their loved ones. He also recorded the entire crew, including himself.

On the thirteenth mission in the thirty days he survived overseas, he shot down an enemy plane while his plane fell from the sky. He did not abandon his post. Instead, he took a plane down with them. The enemy machine-gunned the parachuters and rounded up the survivors, including Robert, who had survived the crash, and machine-gunned them in front of the wreckage.

Robert was twenty-one years old, newly-married to his sweetheart. He left no children to carry his memory. His stricken bride, Louise, refused to keep the ten-thousand dollars of insurance. Instead she insisted that it go to his mother. Robert's love had been enough for Louise.

For the rest of her life, my mother could not bear parades of uniformed men. In my childhood, if the phone rang with no one on the other end, my mother believed it must be Robert, but he was not able to speak. In crowds, sometimes, she thought she saw Robert hurrying away from her because he was damaged or scarred. He had vowed not to come home injured.

He was praised by her as the good soldier who had enlisted before he was called, who was faithful to his duty and accurate to the end but whose potential was destroyed before he could develop as an artist. I took from this that my mission, if I were to be a good soldier, was, somehow, to make up to my mother for her loss of Robert. He is the one I never knew, but his absence has been a large part of my life.

November 11

Colors deepen around flaming maples,
The sun a far off hawk's eye.
A solemn sense of carnage
Descends with evening chill,
Shades of despair of youth, wasted,
The prey of roaring, relentless guns.

They gave themselves for peace elusive,
Intermittent, stolen
Though bought with cash of bone and ash.
A hawk lines its nest with feathers.

Beyond the horizon
A last glow warms slabs of stone,
Row on row, interminable.
Those who held lost ones
In memory are gone.
No one holds their laughs in heart
Or their wounded wailing
Or silent, eyeless grimaces.

The enormity of too-great griefs
Lies sodden in foreign fields
Long ago planted with underground forests
Of casket wood, flesh, bone.

And in my quiet haven I have swept feathers
And spied a hawk spread wings
Against the sky, homeward going,
To the nest warmed with pluckings
From the breast of mourning doves.

Beneath foreign fields the long dead
May be reeling from the battles
They have fought.
What words are worthy of the telling,
The costs, the victories their valor has bought?

Great-Grandmother

Some old women
Have lived beyond the time
When dreams die
And wounds of the heart
No longer weep.
They preside, like temple columns,
Over an arid plain of ruin
And unrestored loss.
Yet they have softened
Like willow withes
In the rains
Of early spring.
They become or have remained
Strongly pliant of the spirit.
They wind their caring,
Like worn ribbons,
'Round those they love
And bind them gently
About with strength.
They are held in memory
And abide in secret clearings
Of the heart
Where they grow into gardens
Of endurance.

Lake Roland

The lyric flow of my life
Goes in the same room
Where nether talkers abide
And pour from their pitchers
Twice-removed sounds,
While I nurture a choice between
Secret wounds or clarity,
A vacancy or fullness
Of a sweet tide.

The Father's house holds
Other chambers,
Running smoothly wide,
Courses and cradle arms
Hinging less on fortuity
Than on seals of dimension
Lapping edges at certain shorelines
Beyond perception.
Flowing is the breaker
Of edges,
Shaper to palm,
Haven of searcher
Where spirit goes wingless
To a loss it needs to gain,
To a lucid sinking of illusion
Through sifting patterns
Ungraspable
As wind carrying
Current on water
In calm, chattering rills
Or in shattering stringlets
Over falls.

My Parents' Music

I listen to the music of my parents' generation.
Their young lives, innocent as sleek plums
Ripening on a tree,
Were early crushed and scraped off the heel of war,
He broken too soon,
She, angry, burdened with a child.
Someone was going to pay
And bear her fears.

Their music, ripe in sentiment and hope
For the fulfillments of peace,
Peeled from static radios
When saber-dishes rattled,
And knives were scraped in our kitchen,
And cuts turned dishwater red,
Suds parting like a livid sea
Over a thorny wilderness of desperation.

Their music seems impossibly innocent,
Thinly quavering over airwaves,
The same currents that comforted GI's in morbid
Straits an ocean away,
My parents perhaps the last generation
When purity was an assumed right of youth
Now plucked too soon,
Now allowed no time of unknowing
And molested by lewd shockings, blood and grit
On every TV or game system.

My parents' music now seems quaint, outmoded, obsolete,
And I hold tenuously to a world half-sensed
And long superseded,
Though I have lived long enough to be a bridge
Between two or three generations,
I am a relic, an alien at home in neither world,
Misplaced, quaint, outmoded, obsolete.

What can I tell the young about the carnivorous world
Where they must make a life?

Throwaways

What they have left me is their trash,
Now, mostly glass,
Clear or brown, still sharp enough
To slice the paws of heedless dogs.
Will some archeologist of an unknown time
Prize these shards the way
Museums or jewelry makers hoard
Roman glass made milky or iridescent by the earth,
Their nether parts eaten
And now, as in my yard, belched up
Digestive rejects, clots, after heavy rains?

I run my thumb along shattered ridges of glass
That trap the glare of sunlight
And offer me markers of seventy years past.
I pluck them, turn them in my hand
And test their points and edges.
Were alcoholics the vanished ones
Who lived on my plot of ground?
There is a harvest of brown bottle slivers.
Why the blue-flowered shards of bowls?
Did they argue and pelt one another with pottery prizes
Gleaned from soap-powder boxes?
Or maybe they were kind and patient. The clumsiness
Of four rowdy children
Can create broken glass scrap piles discarded
In rituals of backyard barrel burning.

I have turned over a time-thinned tin-can lid,
A testimonial to industrial hardiness
Opposing the rude rustiness of time.
A petite white porcelain castor wheel, pristine
In clogged housing was a special find.
Who would burn a side table with feet delicate

As those of a fawn?
What destructive boor would have condemned
It to fires of penitence?
Had it committed the sin of breakage
Under a heavy hand?
Or did someone absolve carelessness
By burning the evidence?
A tiny medicine vial, intact but crusted with clay,
Lay choked amid coal clinkers.
The young of today would be ignorant
Of such phrases.

Once I turned up a perfect, painted pie bird,
Winking its glazed black eye in sunlight and slime,
Interred by a stream.
What brute would bury such a treasure,
The liberator of fruity piecrusts
From steam or its soggy aftermath?

Who would callously dump a knobbed,
Eared, lacy sugar creamer set,
Clear glass stretched to diamond shape?
Had an old lady died and the ingrates
Cast off her small treasures?
I have seen its mates in antique shops,
Saved from watery perdition by foreseeing
Possessors. I have served visitors with this set
Despite one rust stain that would not yield to cleaning.

These vanished people have left me pieces
Of their lives, shards big enough to need
Picking and decisions
But not enough to understand the courses
Of their lives or why
They threw away, discarded untidily,
Relics of their lifetimes
In hints of unsolvable riddles.

Bird Writing

The birds are busy writing
Footprints in the snow,
Punctuating them with beak stabs for seeds.
Their style is cryptic prose
Or poetry of melting images.
Their tracks are story lines,
Generational memories
Of winter songs and yew berries
And stories to tell the nestlings in the spring
Of lovers lost to the hawk
And frost-bitten cousins
Entombed until the thaw
When sullied plumage and crushed lungs
And curled claws
Reveal the unforgivingness of cold.

The yard has become a community bulletin board
For mythologies and lore,
For legends of the hero who intimidated
The raider foxes and raccoons
Or the translator
Who told them what the crows'
Screaming means.
There are tales of wise ancestors
Who could read the weather
Or predict when the robins would return.
There may be warnings
About the grey cat who lurks
In the bare forsythia
Or a list, long as a snowdrift,
About the greed of squirrels
Or not to build a nest
Above the pond
Lest the fledglings drop in and drown

Or to have the young ones tucked abed
Before the owl rouses
To hunt by moonlight.

The mourning dove casts a moving
Shadow on the snow
And on the juncos
Who weigh too little to leave
Their tableaux recorded,
Encrusted in ice,
For the sun to show
Before it erases them.

The jays are absent from the scene.
One message asks who knows
What has befallen them?
Scrapping sparrows crowd the page
With insistent urgencies.
Their diaries are full of exclamation marks
And asterisks.
If they used ink, it would be red,
But the cardinals are reticent.
Color has taught them caution.

The skittish woodpecker
Would rather cry than write.
She flaps and grabs seeds,
Almost hovering.
The starling, preferring anonymity,
Uses green ink
That will mix with the grass.
Some have perfected a hopping style of script.
The custom of right-to-left
Or left-to-right seems optional
In this precinct
Where most seem set
On up-and-down
Or down-and-up notation.

Others prefer a circular
Wandering about the feeder
With enigmas unsolved
And left for the reader.

At The Zoo

All the legs
Disturbed me,
Not those of animals—
The splendid grasp
Of zebra stripe on thigh,
Pristine 'round a muscled hock,
Bones lovely and knobby
Beneath the hide
Doing their job,

But all the human legs,
Mostly women's,
Exposed, touting their wares
Up to the crest of buttock,
Bending over to reveal thong or cheap lace,
The taut, the lean, the flabby, the fat,
All were better covered by some remnant of modesty.

Animals know the inherent decency,
The refined taste of keeping
Their sexual lure discrete,
Not for sale in a market of stares.

Tattoos sprout indelicately,
Trite butterflies and garlanded generic flowers.
What blue ink despondency
To sag obscenely in middle age!

Oh, for the days of sailing ships
That rippled on muscle seas
Or crosses of twined leaves
Bearing "Mother!"
There was honesty
In such simple sentiments,

Some truth of experience,
Not a shabby, fad-some
Superficial search for difference from the herd.
Why not make the yawning gates of hell
On some elbow or tree of life on some knee?

Children squeal or nap
On sweaty adult breasts
Or sag in pouches on the chest,
Infant angelic brows beaded in the heat,
Wisp of halo 'round their ears.

Inert, a giant tortoise
Hangs his head in fouled water.
He is not dead after all
But slurping water through his nose.

The komodo dragon half-smiles benignly and drools,
Claws and elongated toes fleshly sensual,
And presides at a dirty pool.
Alert shifting eyes seem to prize
Us for a meal or diversion.
Streaked glass is our protection
From his lethal kiss.

Between bars, a stealthy monkey grabs a sparrow
And crams it in his mouth.
Mothers gasp, but toddlers
Seem not to notice.
Older boys shout, "Cool!" and "Awesome!"

Pirate vending machines
May cough up liquid
Or frozen sugar treats and keep the change.

Sad gorillas hole up against painted
Jungle walls. Glass enclosed specimens,
They pick invisible nits or prizes infinitesimal

Or non-existent in strewn straw,
Bored, depressed, toys ignored,
Human-like specters of ourselves.
We, too, are caged behind mind-bars
That prize 'humaneness' of captivity,
As we save them from poachers'
Bullets and machetes.

Pigmy goats crowd a low fence.
Thrilled children giggle and pat
Heads and backs,
Amid horn-lets butting,
Until goats flee into a hut
And waste no more attention
On hands found empty.

Two privileged pigs, "Daisy" and "Delilah,"
One appearing dead,
Barely breathe the afternoon away.
The other, half-buried in a wallow,
A plug of snout vibrates mud
In a weak oblivion of satisfaction.

All is tempered by the mob
Of joyous koi
Surging 'round a spitting fountain
In their murky water bed.
Open-mouthed, they tell clueless gapers
A handout is expected now.

Gentle miniature donkeys, bellies bulging,
Line up for a brushing.
A chubby keeper girl astride an exercise ball
Doles out the reward for their passivity.

Two Asian elephants,
Shuffling pillars below land-boat bodies,
Sway and pace on battered clay,

Touch trunks between bars
Then enter their cleaned house
To eat and drink and excrete
On sanitized concrete.
Would they have been more satisfied hauling logs,
Despite the chains and hooks,
Goaded by mahouts,
Had they not been made obsolete
By machinery?
What terminal mindless obstinacy
Of imprisonment taunts them daily?

The panda prowls his emperor terrain,
All the best-- biggest space, exotic trees, grass,
Logs, pool and bamboo. The Chinese cunningly
Deal a hard bargain
For their leased mannequin.

The giraffe, stately on stilts,
Strides across his park
And strains for leaves pruned
Beyond his reach.

Ready to spit, the wily two-hump camel poses stilly,
All hair tufts and dignity
And sand between his toes.

Petulant peacocks strut and flutter
Magic-eye tails
To enchant their ladies.
Their calls, mournful and peevish,
Drone above the human clutter.

Tiger of the fiery eyes paces,
Paces on tawny paws
With unsheathed claws,
Spins and faces us to grin
A silent snarl,
His prison bars imprinted on his hide.

A black leopard embraces a tree
Then wakens to stretch sinuously
And peel scarred bark with his claws,
An unemployed assassin
Meant to glare eyes in the dark.

Half-hidden lions laze and raise
Head or mane
Against the weight
Of crushing afternoon sun.
The theme is "Why bother to parade in scanty shade?"

A rogue rat
Skulks behind a waterlily pond
While mallards preen unconcernedly.
Castoff candy, cookies, hotdog rolls,
Licks of melted ice cream feed him handsomely.
A mangy squirrel scratches and scouts among trash cans
And peanut shells for a prize.

Leaning hard on evening time,
An iron gate slides closed
Until tomorrow's paradise
Reinvents the show.

All Hallows Eve

The day yet to dawn
May be blessed by the martyrdom
Of those who bore arcs of lamplight
For the unreprieved and benighted,

But in these dark hours
When conscience roams in feathers,
Shadowed talons may clutch us
By the shoulder or brush
Wings upon the cheek.
Our wrongdoing assails us in forms
Of fright that clothe guilt in flesh.

We see jackals of deceit
Or the plague-pocked hideously
Grimace, jangle and dance
Toward a smoke-seared purgatory
Lit by flames sulfuriously
From subterraneous caves.
Ghouls escaped are let loose upon the night
As owls blight the moon and shriek.

Black robes rustle in the shadows,
Be they demons or witches casting spells
Who prowl and prey on souls unwary.
Toads that creep upon a crooked path
Lead to covens gathered in groves
Of ancient oaks, their burls mistaken
For clawed watchers, lurking. A cabal
Of chanting looms heavy in damp air.
Strands of mist congeal as horned beasts
Whose green eyes glare at us
In pale lights of swamp gas, vanishing.

If graves, unquiet, spring open, the moaning
And howling that shakes bare trees
May not be wolves of greed
But bereft spirits bewailing un-atoned wrongs,
The lamented legacies of their lives,
And learning what it means to be accursed.

Army Wife

Long since a bride
With girlhood dreams
Of flower crowns, braids and dirndl skirts,
Now, worn and sinewy,
She bends to her work
In a bottling plant.
Strained eyes veiled with glasses,
She finds dirt, chips, cracks
And pulls offending empties
From the moving line.
Queen of rejects, she reigns.

Deep in the American south,
In a treeless trailer park
Scorched, flat and dry,
She co-exists with soldier husband,
No children to prize.
Resting of an evening,
With cool cloths on sore eyes,
She longs for the blessed coolness
Of alpine heights
And her Shepherd shipped from Germany
Who kept her company
These dozen years in husband's promised land,

But Arok, her arrow, Ackie has died
Two, three months since.
He reigns, now, icon-like,
Treasured in a silver-gilt picture frame
She hands tremulously to a visitor,
Offering a mute hope
The image
Can cross a gulf of loss
Broader than the ocean
She has crossed
And comfort
Her girlhood's ghost.

Fifteen Bridges

1. Rusty ones that clank and shudder under thud of cars
   And trucks

2. Others that soar bird-like girder-wings aloft in vacancy
   A prayer passing from one side to another

3. Short-tempered stubby ones that clatter and jostle
   Passers resentfully

4. Double or triple-layered grid work rumblers caging cars
   Within

5. Diesel-dirty oily scrappers over railroad tracks, hub cap
   Snappers
   Crows pecking smashed bubble gum

6. Gothic-spired ones sturdily-girded under grimacing
   Gargoyles

7. Chain-shaking behemoth bridges grinding bedrock to
   Dust
   When tow trucks and semi's lumber over Vulcan's forge

8. Rope and plank spans caught across a gorge

9. Or boards over floating barrels, hemp netting for hand
   Holds

10. Manta-winged ones tethered to pillars footed in deep
    Water
    Ferriers to other fates or toll takers, Charon's helpers

11. Cloud-piercers, tall-towered, painted grey in grey-
    Streaked clouds
    Where the sun stumbles

12. Track-huggers where engines chug, sooted sky above,
    Trash below
    Rats patrolling wasteland

13. Walkers' bridges from muck to muck

14. Raptor-winged perches for fish-preyers

15. Wooden-covered sheds for carriage wheels to run
    Spanners from one era to another.

Rain Driving

Headlights split and splinter
In rain fallen on night roads.
Tires hiss and splatter gathered pools,
Spray the rays of refracted reds
Of signs, neon, that beckon riders
To the yellowed lure of businesses.
Café havens flash violet "OPEN."
Livid neon creatures crawl
Across wavering blacktop
Brilliant in mottled water.
Shaped by the scrape of wiper blades,
Patterns trickle to oblivion,
But beads of blue cling to edges intact.
Streaked greens and ambers command drivers
To go or wait for reflected reds.
Oncoming splashers confuse the code
With winged arcs that shatter in glassy strings
And drum upon the hood.
The car hurtles into blackness, bleak,
Gone strange in dislocation of the dark.
Shadowed hulks consume guardrails,
And yellow lines spring up to bark
The limits of lanes.
"S" messages staked on shields
Caution the treachery of curves.
White center lines weave in rolling sheets.
Drains steam vaporous beasts.
Tree trunks glitter
Where water settles in shagged sheaths
In a maze of bleared beacons
Of prismatic rain.

Road Repair

No Exit

The big yellow eaters chomp and spit
Bits of road-top grit.
Flying ash columns foul innocent lungs.

Road-eaters heave and grind, sigh and choke,
Chewing rough chevron-shaped holes in paving .
The worn road, grown grey, rumbles and squeals
Under whining wheels.

Trapped drivers sweat and curse, lean on horns.
Entitled ones compete and speed on shoulders to escape,
Swing wide over pot holes, swirling gravel, dinging doors,
And break into lanes of those who wait,

While flagmen decree their fate,
Who may go and who must wait,
Indifferent to the waggling hands of clock
Or schedules betrayed.

They scattered cones and jersey walls
Into mazes of bewilderment, blocked lanes,
Miscreated warrens where glass-topped turtles crack.

Blinking orange lights warn
This is the realm of petty kings,
Stogie-mouthed lordlings
In neon-vested robes of state.

Red flags for scepters,
They confer casually on radios,
With the arrogance of those paid by the hour
To make others wait.

They gloat over cones and jersey walls,
Their fiefdom of rush-hour mazes,
Split lanes and traffic snarls

For viewless
Fuming drivers in fuming cars
Blocked in place by semi haulers,
Car-carriers and movers' vans
There is No Exit.

Umbrella

On a narrow spit
Of broad beach, alone, I strode.

To my right, waves
In writhing faces
Of white tearing teeth
Menaced
In ceaseless rows
Like tormented attack dogs
Held in check by a chain of tide.

To my left, the wind, shishing
In my ears, lifted
A horizontal curtain,
A miasmic scrim;
A mist of blown sand
Hurried beyond me
In wavering channels
To some smoky end,

And no one but I
Sought the solace or the threat
Of the baying ocean.

As I raged at the waves
And fumed and prayed
At sinking faces
Over ruthless choices
To be made
There came
An umbrella gaily
Painted in Monet water lilies
Cartwheeling along the waves' edge,
No chasing owner to claim it
Or humble it for its escapade.

I watched, trapped in disbelief,
And woodenly stood,
Envied its lightness
On spokes of feet,
Never sought to halt
Its dash for freedom,

But the wind betrayed
It to the waves.
They made a meal of canopy
And painted grace,
Tore its metal bones
To jagged armlets
And taunted with jutting handle
Struggling, spit up, fought over
By the ravening pack
Of ocean.

All Souls Eve

The dead hold candles for us.
They light them with their essence
And keep vigil
In shrouded, solemn places.

When the flame wavers,
Our breath and theirs comingle,
And every breath leads
Closer to meeting
At the place of their leaving.

Light that has been in their eyes
Kindles warmth in our hearts.
They have bequeathed us mortal shrines
That waver between blight and blessing
With spires of hope
And footings of sand.

They keep counsel in our heartbeats
And watch for our deliverance and healing.
They whisper against our transgressions
And feel a heavy metallic door
Roll inexorably in the track
We have chosen.

Our wick of conscience may cast
Strange shades or shapes
In dark clouds upon the moon
Or echo voices of reproof
In wind sawing through limbs of yew.

And in this night the dead
May be closer
To the veil between us,
Parted then resealed
In the graying dawn.

Arm

In the early 1950's
On a cold day
In a southern city,
On a bus overheated
By the press of bodies,
A young child, I saw
A shriveled figure,
Perhaps a man,
Hunched, withering
Within a big black overcoat.
I pictured a crow on stilted legs.

The bus lurched, and he reached
To grab the rail.
His sleeve slipped to bare a pale
Underside of arm
Stained by numbers, dark,
Block-style, industrial
Debasing or enshrining that sinewy arm.

I was ignorant of his history,
Yet I could feel it was ominous, dark.
Chilled, I hunched to hide
Within my coat.
I knew he was a pilgrim in flight
From a benighted world.

Angels Of The Dawning Hour

Angels of the dawning hour
Billow in the air
In full glad circles,
Riding on the breath of souls,
Their sounding trumpets
Hidden in the pause between heartbeats
Or in the songs of birds.

In all the currents of dark hours,
Couched in clouds,
They have been patient in their watch.
They ride in tides that cover a radiant moon,

But they arise unbidden
Before the sun transcends
The bounds of distant hills
And carry with them blessings
To disperse upon the slumbering earth.

In their flowing vestments
That sway to music beyond hearing,
There is a faint edge of rustling
Wings and feathers
Or satin laced in starlight
In rippling folds,

And in rain they softly fall,
On every tender petal an embrace.
They are sensed in cleanness of the air
And are breathed inward in a moment
When the heart cries
In solemn silence
For the sweetness it enfolds.

Ferns In Stone Walls In Edinburgh

They have taken hold
And made stone their own
Where pageantry and want
In the slow drain of history
Are screamed by arcing gulls.

Shadows find their place
In hollows between stones
With ferns whose roots
Have caressed gaps in solidity,
Combed and tended rain,
Dew and errant soil.

Stairwells, drains secretly
Give refuge, abet them
In their purpose
Of bringing life,
Although unwanted,
To centuries of shade.

They are staunchly green
And spring to the touch.
Lichen and moss befriend them
As do sprays of violet bloom,
Though mainly they are friendless,
Unnoticed, uncherished
Yet vibrant.

Gulls Around Holyrood

They bully, bark and howl
Like mobs of demented children,
Prowling late into the summer night
When darkness fails to fall.

They defy the voiceless moon
And screech into the roofless
Reaches and scattered tombs
Of the abbey ruin

Whose forlorn stone shoulders
Bear windowless eyeholes
And arching arms
Enfolding centuries of gloom.

The ravening gulls
Like taunting demons
Go besieging graves and stealing
Whatever peace the dead may claim.

Who could better summon souls
Beneath their slabs
To pace and crunch the gravel
On the abbey floor

Where ruptured stone coffins
Lay strewn as if forewarning
The Day of Judgment
Or of Doom?

Who could better echo
Rizzio's wailing pleas
When mercy was a stranger
In the Queen's chamber

Where jealousy and scheming
And knives and bleeding
Left faded stains
Upon the boards?

Who could better fly
To heaven the prayers
Of souls entombed while living
To seal against the plague

Whose avengers day and night
Are screaming in the skies,
Haunting the sleeping
With tormented dreaming?

Who could better shriek, "Remember!
Remember!" than the beggars
Or the raging warriors
On the wing,

Whose weapons are but feathers
And whose trumpets are but weeping,
Maddened echoes in the closes
And walls of haunted stone?

Ardchattan Priory – 800 Years

Shadows fall long
In evening that struggles to come.
A gate encloses arches of stone.
Walls are gone, stolen,
A church become a graveyard
In long-enduring Scotland.

The Lochnell Aisle remains,
Ancestors below sinking slabs,
Names fading, worn.
Some cannot be read or known
In the slow decay of rock on bone.

None but ruin here holds sway,
And across the way
Is a loch, a firth, a bay.

Here spirits may claim
Their own preserve and roam
Or pray, "Who owns the night?"
Answered by haunted voices
From a dovecote
Calling the dark to come.

Cold Beach

After empires of heat
The cold beach challenges me.
Wind eats at my resolve.

The pearled sky vies
With vastness of the sea,
While in the west loom
Leaden clouds,
Consuming hints of sun.

The grey Atlantic collides
In steely sheets,
Upended, rhythmic, rootless
In goadings of unseen moon
And dismal as a dream
From which is no wakening.

A troop of gulls
In ruffled ranks
Claims a spot of beach
To rest, nestled in sand,
Guarded by one-legged veterans
With worn feathers
Who stand, planted
In the flux of water,
Wind and sand.

The Damaged Tree

The men are destroying the damaged tree.
Their saws burn angrily
Into the heartwood where sap flows,
And leaves, like dresses, spill to earth
Or like scabs or crusts, fall away.

The heart bleeds sap or tree blood.
Dismembered limbs drop and jar the earth.

Birds flee and are silent
In their mourning.
Doves will later cry
Their losses,
A hundred years of shelter,
A hundred years of grandeur.

There is no mercy from
Helmeted men.

Excavation

Today I got the news:
There is to be another
Excavation
In my small sagging
Mountain.
It reminds me that
My stone-carving teacher would say,
"What's all this digging?"
When he viewed my sorry chiseling
Like tooth marks gnawed around a block
Broken from a mountain.
He, with amusement, would look
From eyes that knew
The reasoned slicing
Of stone, flesh-like and yielding.

Now, I am fearful
In my all-too-failing flesh:
The offending trail of white spots
Must be brought to answer
For their intrusion
And their secrets stripped
Like understory trees
On a domed and doomed mountain.

Strip miners sharpen the teeth of their blades
To chew and eat stones and earth, roots,
Fodder for the feasting of their machines,
And some nameless one sharpens and polishes
The surgeon's shiny scalpels.

The mountain will lose its dome,
Scar-like roads eating their way to its flattened top,
And I, who knows?

My case is nothing special.
I am just another chain link
In a rotation of gnawing teeth,
Just another notch on the handle
Of a scalpel,
And this is just another trail of smoke spots,
An alarm call,
From the fire spotter's outpost
On mortality mountain.

Before Cancer

Before cancer
There is one life,
But terror and anguish remold the self
Into one focused on fragility.
The body recoils from brutal choices
While the mind witnesses and shrieks in disbelief.
Mutilated, scarred, the body,
Sickened by treatment, poisoned from within,
Struggles against its limits.

The spirit seeks wholeness and balance
Between hope and the choke hold of mortality,
Once a distant inevitability,
And now sensed at the shoulder, exhaling, waiting.
It distrusts the body's treachery
And mourns that reprieve is temporary.

The new life seeks gratitude for the mercies
And miseries of treatment
And reorders what is meaningful.
Old sorrows do not fade
But are laid against a changed measure.
The days that follow are shaded by their brevity.
The self, betrayed, has lost careless belief in health
And listens with apprehension to its heartbeat.

The Body Mourns

Solace hides beneath boulders
In caves of the mind.
Emotions seep in raw edges
Of wounds. The flood of uncapped veins
Is staunched by sutures that pick the heart.
The body is a wordless keeper.
It is not swayed by logic
Or consolation.

It mourns loss of parts
And weeps in secret cells
Where blood keeps conversation
With deeper impulses of being.
Cells know their fellows are gone
And clamor for restoration, for healing
In blind alleys of regeneration.

The body knows what wholeness means:
To be sleek as a red-coat fox
Trolling in a meadow,
And it mourns
Deep in a salt mine of the spirit
And is trapped where eager borers
Tunnel and shatter its integrity.

There is no logic in loss.
A dying fox quivers in underbrush.

Knight's Progress

I came to Camelot
To serve my master,
But I gave my trust
To another man's wife.

I pledged my purity
To my lady Queen,
And I found silken sheets.

I came to Camelot
To be true of heart,
And I placed a dart
Between shoulder blades.

I came to serve honor,
And I learned that intrigue
Weaves white blankets of reprieve.

I came with a sword to serve truth,
And I saw crows
Peck out a dead man's eyes.

I came with a conscience as buckler,
And I learned it is a fool's cup
With a bottom that leaks.

I came for humility,
And I learned hardness of heart
In the splendor of silver banners.

I came to lend might to justice
And I found scalp and skull
In the belly of a serpent.

I came to seek permanence,
And I saw that castles
Are clouds on mountain tops.

I came for fellowship,
And I learned to hide a dagger
In my stocking.

I came in peace,
And I pierced bone
With my lance.

I came with a gauntlet to grasp enemies,
And I caught one
In the looking glass.

I learned the most high among men
May be unraveled
By a thread of truth.

I played chess on a beach
With one in black robes
Who conquered my reason and hope
With artfulness.

He felled my vigor
With a winding sheet
And laid my shield over me.

Labor Day

They labored
Men eaten by machines
Factory whistle for elegy
Their souls laid out on conveyor belt or assembly line

The incessant clattering looms demanding thread
Never sufficiently fed
Brown lung lint sickness for mill women and children

Black lung miners' reward for shoveling pearls
On plates of masters
The pursuit of coal turned men and boys to moles,
And the company store stole wages

They labored
Where pick axes clawed the earth or flinty mountains
Gutted for tunnels
Where men hacked the hearts of ancient forests
And unrooted hillsides spilled into rivers and cities

Where oxen stumbled, men or women pulled
Plows and baled
Where cotton bolls soaked up finger blood
And sun and heat bent backs and numbed brains
Where fields of cane lashed back at slashing knives
Where a surfeit of trees – apple, plum or peach
Mocked their need

Where coffin ships spit out the famished and diseased
Where women in squalor gave birth to fodder
For looms, presses and stampers to consume
For domestic drudges to trudge flights of stairs
To empty chamber pots for the wealthy
Where drones in sweatshops stitched and prayed
For unused air

Where great iron-hearted locomotives panted and roared
Whose freight whistles stung the souls of men,
Men whose hammers beat tracks into orderly submission
Where jobless tramps rode whining
Rails to thankless destinations
And fled the prairie dustbowl

Where 18 wheelers smacked the highways
Down to a humming song
Amid gasping airbrakes
Where men climbed girders to the sky
As wind flapped their pantlegs

Where men blasted, dug and built to trick rivers in to dams
And drown the rivers' soul
Where men stole mountain tops from the Smokies

Where men in boats weighed their nets with fishes
Given by waves and storm

They labored.

Nocturne

In the light of every darkness
That enfolds me,
My shape is one
With shadows
While all about me stream
Beacons of light,

And through dimensions
That close about me
Like sliding doors,
I pass and leave
Imprints of longing
Embedded in tracks of sand
Toward a shadowed barque
Moored on a lapping sea,

And who I am
Rustles like a soft dove
Bedded among damp leaves
In branches that sway
In currents like the sea,
Feather breast spread
To encompass
Small wonders
And nestlings
Under wings
Sheltered.

Through dust
That glows
In motes suspended
In shafts of light
Between this place
Or time, undefined,
My being slips
Like breath spent,
Unnoticed.

If Goats Howled

If goats howled
And the moon were darker
Than the night sky,
And fish crawled upon treetops,
Humming as they went,
Or horses decreed a day of amnesty
For all that waddle, trot or swim,
If trees beckoned to sloths,
Or candles shielded moths,
If snakes wove a trellis
To make a shaded bower,
Or the osprey's golden eye courted the sun,
If wandering were a gateway
To some fuller senses,
And feathers wove a carpet of innocence
For those that part the sky,
If clouds caressed the shore in frothy splendor,
Or vultures fed on clover,
And lions herded dolphins,
If doves bayed at the moon in nightly sorrow,
And wolves and eagles trumpeted
A reign of peace,
Or elephants rejoiced in rumbling voices,
Then creatures' cackling, calling,
Howling, baying, bawling
Would sing the sweetest harmony
Unknown to man,
And ears and minds, unstopped,
We would understand.

Grey Reservoir

After brilliance has past,
And the rapture of colors has dulled,
Somber trees are bared
To winter's blighted blast.

Geese have homed to softer climes,
Though strays have lingered
On ragged shores in grey patrol, entranced.
Oaks and hickories beyond stands
Of muted pines, burls and boles,
Trunks and limbs outstretched
To grasp some ethereal source.

Greyness seems everlasting
As if a farther depth or soul
Abides below water shelves
Or searches taproots of trees.

A fortress among rocks gives shelter
To souls as if sprung from them
In granite strength conceived
To bear the grated rasp of trials
Or droughts that deplete the will.
A dull march of days and troubled nights,
Bears the water depths upon themselves.

Below this weight the soul quests
In stirring currents
For some endless life spring
In eternal, onward, homing press.

Nepenthe

As rain bedims the dawning hour
The rush is louder
Than birds who have forgotten songs.

The growing light enforms solidity
Of trees, cars, houses
That guard those who sleep or dream within.

The land retreats from darkness
And a vagary of forms,
Though rain would hold a cup to night
Then pour and soften hard edges
Or lave them in forgetfulness,

And what has gone before or yet may come
Trails to whispered ends
Or dreamers' sighs,

But in the lull of misted thought
Or idled will,
When breath has settled on sleepers' eyes,
Shadows weave between fallen doors
And leave no more than slips of rain.

Twelve Autumn Haiku

Deepest red blood leaves
Lay a mantle on the earth
Soon a cold embrace

Sifting leaves red gold
Whipped and chased by wind and chill
Ladybug flees lost

Brown leaves wind blasted
Heaped upon stone wall
Green moss endures an ice crust

Cold sun on bright leaves
Fading red gold brown
Footsteps rustle on cold ground

Wind blast bird pecks ice
Big Coat person hurries by
Eating shares no crust

Footsteps crush brown leaves
Red and yellow soon falling
Geese on wing calling

Winged vee's in sky geese
Homing for the reservoir
Staying to greet ice

Clamorous geese sky
Barking warning while leaves die
Soon snow feathers fly

Squirrel digs for nut
In leaves red gold brown
Long winter cold only friend

One red bird crying
Picks through fallen leaves
No red one to answer him

Last leaves shrivel on branches
Brown ones rustle under foot
Sunless sky

Evergreen keeps faith
Cold birds nestle in
Bare trees awaiting new crown

Over-Ripe Lady Haiku

Over-ripe lady
Struts in too-tight clothes
Bandages on broken hopes

Black-dyed hair teased big
Crowds a puckered face
Talon-eyes seek lucky love

Heels too high make wobble gait
Gaudy jewelry
Neck-snake for paste face

Brass tarnished ear hoops
Big lonesome glass cocktail ring
Strong perfume repels

Old fur cape dead fox
Spreads stale closet smell
Eager lady bar stool watch

Crossed-leg foot wiggle
Wags shoe heel on off
Sends warning iron trap snap

Codger Haiku

Codger saggy seat
Pucker lip stubble
Snag-tooth snarl acid breath

Cold coffee and canned dog food
Greased hair torn bed sheet
Broken clock face glares

Newspapers in heaps
Hope wilts and wallpaper peels
Dirty laundry stinks

Cracked piano stool
Brass tarnished frame holds captive
Smeared windows for soul

Lady lace collared
Trapped in frame stares drearily
Codger's own trophy

Young Girl Haiku

Young girl bud piercings
Lip nose ear navel
Unripe peach blight frost or fire

Pink-painted nails bite
Hair streak bleached straw-like
Holes cut in jeans heart tear bleeds

Ring hung on neck chain
From pretend boyfriend
Weigh scale skip meal eat ice cream

Misplaced self stare at mirrors
Seek clue of lost one
Thick eye-blue makeup

Wan self seen in shop window
Seems dimensionless
Pierced again scar fresh

Loud music drowns dread
Sunflower-self seeking praise
Flattered with light rays

Easy to misuse
Girl ardently accepts mere
Tokens from takers

Young Boy Haiku

Young boy rock skipper
Pond and stream stepper
Dreams of sailboat army planes

All things that hover
Fly above dull land
Climb mountain ride rocket free

Scrawny legs thin arms
Climb rope and conjure tree house
Jungle explorer

Magic wanderer
Fort builder back yard
Game time in sheet tent flash lit

Young Woman Haiku

Young woman half moon rocker
Silver tide night flow
Slender limbs gliding

Willow arms cheek smooth
Long hair glistens sways
Skin breathes night trees respiring

Hand touch gentle cling
Embrace a cloud fold
Night hums promise longing old

Laughter hush past smile
Untouched heart eyes trust
Dreaming moth flight leaf unfolds

Life promise keeper
Blue shadowed lake depths unseen
Completion seeking

Unknown fullness self
Birth giving within
Chrysalis break opening

Treasure self rain bud
Root stem spreading vine
Soon green and tender presence

Sentinel Crow's Song

No one thanks a sentinel
For cawing alarms
To those who hold nestlings
Under their breasts,
To all who scatter
And hide in the brush,
Alerted, a-tremble,
Knocking breath withheld,

Who cares for our merit,
Dive-bombing the hawk?
We fly angry armadas,
Vengeful as sea gods.
We gang in a rabble
And screech, harass that pillager
Pirate to leave our garden intact.

No one notes the oiled sheen
Of our coats, feathers whispered afloat.
We patrol the sky
And guard the inner coastlines
Of our turf.

The glint in our eyes
Is a gift of the sun.
Preened and correct,
We strut our steps.
Our pride shows.
Militant for those of beak and wing,
We dare the hawk to return
Or pierce our skies
With hunter's claws.

To Depression

You know the downs of down, the doors of mood
And the grey slidings on the scales of
In between.

You know the inner conflagration,
And the charred fragments of spirit, falling ashes
And the flaying of the soul.

You know the flattened dullness of days
Bearing down heartlessly,
And the slow clock
That pours itself down
The throat of night
To half-restoring sleep.

You know the mud walls
Of the pit
And the claw holds
To get out
And the collapsing clods
Of earth, broken fingernails.

You know the loss of wings,
The longing to rise, cloud-like
To sun rays streaming within,
Yet you keep a jailer's hold
And turn a key
In your lock.

Sleeper (Wasteland-Scape)

Like twin plateaus
His chest rose,
Softened by a brush of hair,
And fell with breath expended.
His shoulders were my sunset,
Twin cups to pour a sunrise
Left unpoured behind closed eyes.
His arms at rest
Beside his chest
Were blunted steps of pyramids.
His hands in fists
Were faces of a sphinx
Whose slow eroding cast
Grains of sand
On barrenness,
While he, blanketed, a mystery
Or half-found presence
That obdures in stone,
Slept on,
And I, a watcher, touched
Only with my eyes
A grace constrained
Within his face.

December Beach

Whipped racing coils of waves
Form leaden crests
Heaving on the beach.
Foam makes laced fans
At my feet.

Crests transform to warriors
In chariots, careening.
They whip horses screaming
Then receding, flinging manes
Dissolved in froth.

Pitted prints of the vanished
Leave pockmarks in sand.
The grey Atlantic claims land
As the pull of moon allows.
Few gulls, sentries, claim outposts.
They brace against wind bite
And scatter as I pass.

The forlorn sun wavers in a mirror
Of iridescent sand
Scoured by raging waters.
Clouds, black as sea wrack,
Track across a vast sky
And tear holes in light
That offers no respite
From the cold.

Sequencing

Wood thrush, pin-feathered, is rebuffed
Amid scrapping sparrows, strutting crows and screeching gulls
When bread is thrown
In the decayed city center

Where drunks and dispossessed sleep rough
On park benches
Where junkies trade and pimps prosper
Where madmen throw lice at passers by
And gaping eyeholes of ruined warehouses
Stand guard against revision.

The wood thrush dodges cats and rats, trucks
And brick throwers.

Next day, it tries harder but is too weak to win a crumb.

Next day, it is crippled, one foot curled up,
Flapping wings that will not lift it.

Next day, it is not to be seen in the rabble
Of scrabbling beaks and wings.

Meanwhile, four miles away, an aged lady wheels
Her chair to the window at the end of a hall
In a nursing home.
She has abandoned television, Bingo and crafts
To stare for hours at trees and unfurling leaves.
She confides, "This is my heaven!"

Meanwhile, nine miles away, a daughter waits her turn
For the radiation machine.

Dragon

I am the green of fertility and vigor.
I spin in air waves
And twist in cloudscapes.

I fly; I soar in the wind embrace,
And the sun that warms my belly
Becomes my crown, thunder bolts my scepter.

With my claws, I pull down clouds
And scoop waves from the sea
To meet where I reign.

I drag the living rain
To the land where people plead
For sustenance of their crop.

They thank me in the season of growing
That I have blessed the skies
With seeds of rain.

I stir the growth of grain
With the streams of my breath.
I am mighty but gentle. That is true power.

I throw boulders of snow
And scatter them with my wings
Into flakes that shelter the earth with my presence.

My eyes see the wrongdoing of men,
And I chasten them with my lips
That nip their souls.

My shadow is opacity in dark water
Until I rush the air into currents
Seen on water glinting.

Thunder is the clapping of my wings
And, distant, is the far echo of bells or cymbals.
I waft the smoke and fragrance

Of their incense through the temple to bless them.
Old men in saffron robes, their lives spent
In prayer and chanting

May spy the tip of my wing, my gift to them.
How the harmony of music riffles my feathers!
When I arch my back, the rainbow forms.

Scales of my spine
Make prisms of color
Revealed in facets of varied shining,

And when I coil around the moon,
Clouds seem to chase the lonely light
Until the sun reveals my splendor.

Current

The chop of water sways
To eternal necessity,
A pushing or pulling away
Of a grand attractant.
Grey caps on dark risers
Surge from blacker troughs
In fleeting ranks
Of risen ridges, angled,
Receding, at once replaced
By cross movers gaining
A surface the wind allows
And depths disgorge.
They, too, march in liquid divisions
And vanish in constant progress, repeating
A pattern overlaid as one submerges and is gone.
They cross contend for a moment's supremacy
And weave between one another,
Braiding a water rope
Or yoke of mastery where storms clash
Toward some crashing end
A half-world or farther
In wracking swells soon tamed
To sifted rivulets on harrowed sand.
Lone specks on heaving vastness,
Birds easily ride the buffeting.
As if crowned, they bathe, regally preen
And flick their feathers
And peer for prey.
Others in the stiller parts or tidal pools
Dip their necks, slip between wavelets
And disappear to depths
Where currents form and collect.

The Soul Of Land

The soul of land, as of a whisper heeded,
Rises in faint vapors, mists.
Through a density of rock, clay, sand,
A current of life passes,
Bearing underground rivers, streams
For the taproots of trees.
The soul, quiet matron, rests beneath stars,
Fulsome, generous to seedlings and striplings
Whose growth impels them, hissing,
To break the surface.
Her breast is laid open by plow or furrow,
Scarred. Her deep pulse
Throbs through molten chambers
Of melted stone churning upward
To burst and sear her spine with new land
Soon claimed by windblown seeds, weeds,
Decomposing stone, bone, shells.
A filter of past beings,
Her density is a shield from light
And casts a dampness that welcomes, exhales
Some ancient memory of dust, tomb-like.

The Cost Of Youth

I.
From the remove of later years
The names of old war dead
Seem remote, their causes sometimes archaic,
Their credos, sometimes so simplistic
As to seem whimsical
That men believe and inflict horrors
On their fellows in causes that devour them.

Wars to end wars engender future wars.
Victims become martyrs
To rouse more and more vicious revenge
And more martyrs.
There is no end to cruelty
Or beastliness more beastly
Than beasts in their innocence could imagine.

In the abyss of human depravity
Heroes are born and often die dutifully, unremarked,
Patiently like beasts led to slaughter pens,
Not knowing if their sacrifice
Will engender peace
Or justice that often does not prevail,
And what is left to uplift, to inspire?

II.
For these, the inheritors, the young
It is always a new world,
No matter how debased or strumpeted,
Their era most significant,
Their tasks of life more urgent.
The assumption that all is possible
Seems real and attainable to them.

Those who have lived long can admire the innocence
And wince for the vulnerability of the young.
Self-serving leaders pander to their gullibility,
The young who have never paid
For anything, and assure them
That government largesse is free
And is owed to them.
One can smile at the arrogant
Certainty of the young
That they know more
And are brighter, more capable
Than their elders who have been tried by struggle.
It is possible to hope the young will do better
Although it is not likely.

Hawk

When I soar, the wind caresses my feathers.
The sun rides on my shoulder.
I tilt my leads to catch the drafts
That raise me.
I mount the currents to wheel and dive.
The wind is a servant, and I, its master, bend
It to my will.

I, mighty in the wind throe,
Spy below all the small, dull and slow
Who cannot heave themselves into a wind glide.

From aloft, I catch the glint in the sparrow's eye
From where it hides.
The mouse, the vole are helpless in my thrall.
The dove mourns no more within my talons' grasp.
I savor the crunch of bone that oozes marrow,
The grainy grind of gristle
And strings of sinew on my breath.
I thrill to tear my beak
Into bleeding meat, its hook and edge, the point
Sharp as my eye.
I hear panting heartbeats
Under leaves that quake,
And I strike to the quick.

I am not burdened with pity or remorse.
In the preening of my wings
And the honing of my claws
I rejoice.

Talk To Me

Tell me about your inner wars,
The ones that scour your guts,
The blades in your heart,
The ones that riot in the morning,
Shades against the innocent sun,
And haunt you in the midnight hours,
Forms stealing across night lights.

Tell me about the wrongs done to you
That demeaned your worth
And the wrongs you have done,
Thoughtlessly and on purpose,
When you took spite in someone's pain
Though you have denied or explained
White feathers on brown sodden fields,

And amid that falling,
You could not cry the deepest wounds,
The secrets hidden in your soul,
Furrowed ruts in melting ice,
But the silent time at dusk in snow
Wounds you yet again.

Reply:

I have waged a life,
A campaign to be as I desired,
And I have faltered,
Not as gravity sinks a stone
In dark water,
But elusively, as I have seen fields,
Plowed, damp, brown,
Coated in rime
In the first days of winter.

I have felt ice in my spine
When the ardor of living
Shudders against the coming of hard frost,
And whatever spring may rise
Lies locked in seeds
Upheaved in the first thaw.

Northwest Coast Indian Masks

At the museum, under glass,
Masks I saw:
Fiercely focused birds who crack
The skulls of men
And drain their brains.
A wolf I saw
Whose toothful grin
Opened to the bird within,
And a man-face would open
To a woman
Except that she is missing,
Uncollected, roaming
Unshamaned in nether
Voids of spirit,
And she, a mask hollow-headed
From felled log,
Remains lost or haunted between
Terrors or benignities
I, too, may have seen.
And later, on film I saw
A sleep-broken woman
Draw her lover's back
Against her chest
And caress him with her fingers.
A tenderness in finger-kisses
Play-acted for a camera-mask
Evoked in me a feeling
That seemed real in heart and throat,
Yet I cannot say in what spirit-dreaming,
Or if, I have lived this feeling.

Georgia S.O.P.

It was Georgia,
The town of Columbus,
(Named for the opener of the New World),
Christmastime, 1960.

All the black soldiers,
On leave from serving their country,
Were herded into the cramped "Colored Waiting
Room"
Of the Greyhound station.
Isolated, they could not hear boarding calls.

They waited long hours
While workers loaded bus
After bus after bus
Of white soldiers and civilians,
Bound for home and family
To celebrate the birth
Of the Giver
Of New Life.

Pronunciation In Georgia

In Columbus, 1960,
All the white people
Named "Jordan"
Pronounced it "Jurdan"
As in the "Jordan Mills,"
And all the black people
Named "Jordan"
Pronounced it "Jordan"
As in the river
To be crossed.

Toilet Codes In Tennessee

Knoxville, 1962,
One department store,
Choice of two restrooms,
The Ladies' or the Women's,
Chose the closer.

Emerged from stall
To find two
Black women
Glaring at me.
I had invaded
The Women's Room.

Section Six

Sonnets

Wick Cutter

I.
When the candle melts
And the wick has given of itself,
Someone comes with a knife
To cut the wick
And trim the spent ashes,
Crumbled in the hand to stains of soot,
With no more thought or feeling
Than for any used-up thing,
Though this one has given light
And severed night into manageable arcs.
It gave a path through darkness
And reduced fear or lostness
Into shadows with no more power
Than to haunt the spirit.

II.
This is a feat for a small piece of string.
It might have been saved
If it had bound a mundane package
Or a sheaf of musty letters.
If it had not given brightness,
It might have been retained.
Stains on darkened fingers
May be wiped clean,
But in the pores and whorls
Some residue remains
And in turn soils
Crisply laundered napkins,
And that cutting, that crushing remain
'Though wax and string have vanished.

Amphion

I.
My lyre is tuned to the weight of stars
And the pull of the luring moon.
The sun begets my melody
For my notes are strung on gold
In chords of perfect harmony.
It is not magic that sways the stones
To lift, to cling, to lock in place a wall.
They hear with crystal ear
And feel in their pores
The ageless song that all creation loves,
That all creation breathes
And the vacancy of space craves
Then hurls its broken, longing rocks
To earth in showers of burning light.

II.
If stones in their density
Follow songs of the lyre
And transport themselves to chords
That trail upon the air and flow together
In the joining of rocks and mortar,
If stones are porous to the rise of notes,
How much more can the human heart
Be uplifted by this same melody?
If stones find harmonies
Within their crystal pores
And obey some fire-brimmed urge for unity
From the magma of their core,
Then how might the spirit
Burn for melding into one?

October

I.

Wind is whisking through the trees
With all the breath of souls parted from the sun
That inflames the leaves in gold, red or dun.
Shadows lunge from plunging tree arms
Pulled and shoved by swirling gusts.
Whirling leaves trouble spirits with no reprieve.
Wind, more owl-like, moans as trunk
Wears on trunk, wearily rubs coils of currents.
Green retreats to the last hold of summer
And bares its shaken sheaths
To light that searches through limbs,
Settles on the earth and raggedly crowns the turf.
Shadows blot the sun cast on green lawns.
Crows presume to bargain with the lost.

II.

A flight of shadows proclaims the fall
While the wind bites and claws
And rakes forsaken leaves
In grave-like mounds beneath stark trees,
A harsh reprieve for whatever spirits roam.
Last tapestries are stolen from the sky
When color has fled and whispers moan
The loss of long-light August heat.
A wary owl patrols the night
When mice and voles are hidden
Within a brown wasteland
Of shattered remnants,
Scraps of this year's promise
Swept away in cold demise.

White Night

I.

When crowns of silver settle
As circlets in the snow
Or gold glow arced by radiant street lamps
And blend sleep with wakeful guardians,
Night yields to heavy weight of snow
While minions of the mind teem
In troublous dreams
Then wake to white forgetfulness.
Over blanketed streets where cars creep
And few have wakened,
The spirit raises above
Falling flakes and surveys
A weightless kingdom
Seen or sensed beyond veils of seeming.

II.

A realm trance-like inhabits the mind
With a presence of the day past
Or the one yet to come.
The spirit, strangely adrift,
Senses that it is not contained by either one
And that its home or origin
Is less weighty than flakes of snow
Yet more real than flesh,
More permanent than melting frost,
And as night pales
Into an enchanted day
Made mysterious by whiteness,
Dreams recede into wakefulness
That is less aware and less prescient.

One Small Light

I.
As morning fell or rose from the earth,
Steely, cold and grey,
One light, sentinel in dark hours,
In the night, a guardian,
Witnessed or averted shapeless threats
Then paled and weakened.
Overrun by the force of day,
Night retreated from the fray.
Heralded by croaking crows,
Dawn's first champions,
Bearing ashen shields.
Across the field light strode,
Goliath-like, a warrior,
And slew the dark's one comforter.

II.
If a light may weary
From the gift of making clear,
From the work of ridding fears
That fade in darkness,
Then failing is a triumph,
Of vigor rightly spent
In the spread of solace lent
From one small source,
And if the shades of dread
Have had their course
And clung to shattered armor
Or tattered shirts of mail,
Then dreamers or the wakened
Put on helmets of the day.

Veils

I.
Although the earth lies under snow,
Stilled, inert, silent-seeming,
The pale sun of winter pauses
Among brooding branches to prod
A pulse of life,
A ray upon a shuttered shrub,
A pilgrim bud uplifted amid fallen timber,
The litter of last year's leaves, splintered,
Staining the shadowed frost.
Rocks protrude, one side whitened,
A boulder obdurate, aged beyond aged
Remains a fortress crystalline
Surviving beyond dying,
Proof against invasive time.

II.
Frost, snow and rain fleeting
Masks and veils upon the earth,
Beneath the surface beating
A heart alive beyond a heart,
Imprisoned in a chest,
Attuned to pulse eternal
Throbs in joy supernal.
The everlasting new creates old dews
And fallen tears under human soles
Treading on the heart beneath them.
Obdurate as the rocks men stumble,
Unknowing, unwise in restless lives,
In sorrow, loss or unfilled hope.
Amid tears or veils upon the earth they cope.

Plastic Bag

Above, a plastic bag snagged in barren tree
Is shredded in the wind
And in spiked branches, tormented.

Below, ivy clutches and digs
Into seams of faded shingles,
Shrouds a window air conditioner,
Fretfully fingers a satellite dish.
An open window heats the winter cold.
Shutters, unhinged, flap and bang in gusts,

And in a grassless yard, two white
Shirts splayed on sagging line,
Guard a seedless feeder.
Someone has hacked a privet
To scalp a hedge in line.

The Sea Holds Hostage

The sea holds hostage
Broken collars of the land.
Frenzied fingers of flame
Explode, escape the deeps, hissing, ranting
To the surface and proclaim
The abundance of fire, the force to make
New land to join the old
Or ring it in hollow holds
Of palm-shrouded atolls.
The magma of colliding giants
Hurls plates against mountain walls
And thrusts them to the empty sky
While underneath, liquid land
Boils and rages to flee chains of the sea.

Rough Hands Of The Sea

The sea holds in rough hands
Those that venture among high-flung crests
And cradle themselves in treacherous beds
That rock them in gentleness
Or heave them in troughs of riotous waves
That collapse upon them in drowning rests.
From a moaning cradle, a lullaby of lapping
Turns to maddened roars
When stars are vanquished
And cast no ghosts upon the waters,
And the moon retreats in shrouded clouds,
When creatures of the deeps have sounded
To breachless depths
And ride in peacefulness.

The Sleeping Soul Of Land

I.
The soul of land lay open
Spread wide upon the earth,
Awaiting the gift that night has laid
To rise and flourish,
To climb the empty air
And greet the sky.
The grey of morning,
Not yet nacre or pearl,
Not yet streaked or streamered
In the uprush of vital sun,
Is hushed but for chanting birds
Restless for the dawn,
Imploring the light to come
And nourish the waking ones

II.
To feed the fields,
The foxes and fawns,
To bud the oaks,
The sycamores and gums
And gladden the bees to stir
For the sake of all that grows,
To urge the falcon to flight
Or the owls to mourning places
For those that hide from light
Or retreat to caverns of night,
To cause the grain to ripen ears or awns,
To flood the rivers with coursing brightness
And raise the dawning soul
Replenished in darkness.

Fiery Soul Of Land

The soul of land is fiery
Though obscured in rocks, mud and sand.
The core burns in frantic vitality,
Restless, roiling in molten pools,
Striving to uprise.
Veins burst forth in flaming tracery
And burn new land upon the old
And give birth to fire that sears the earth
With black, liquid, livid stone
Seething to the sea
In clouds of luminescent steam,
With pangs of groaning,
Parting from the deep
Wells of fearsome life.

Tall Grass

As tall grass is beaten flat
By rain and wind,
Trampled by beasts or men
Yet rises again toward the sun,
So is the spirit fluid,
Seeking its own currents,
And lifts upon
The rolling meter of hope
And grows like grass
In every seam or crack of that
Which would seal it
Or decry the longing to be
Which lends form to mutability
Yet obscures the flow of constancy.

Ancient Oak

The ancient oak is casting off its limbs,
Stripping to its heart.
Brittle branches snap and grab
Hands that would gather them.
Scant living sap for blood
Seeps through its core.
Splintered arms, broken across the grain,
Are shattered, pale, sapless remains
With sickly mold where red mites patrol.
The bulk of trunk is wrapped in ragged sheets of bark,
Stained in winters' sunless flank.
Rotting leaves prepare a bed
For its hard fall in winter or the spring
When new buds are withering.

Burying Ground

Sorrows of the world by man or nature begot
Are heavy-laden on wide spread arms
That bear flower garlands, carved, or crowns
Of troublous spheres, unmended in years forgot.
Tangled towers of ancient oaks and yew
Loom with bell-rung spires
And tombs stone angels topped.
A hawk cries in churchyard, harries rabbit, deer or fox.
Tears have watered green grounds,
Lent names to straw strewn on fresh mounds,
Once dear to those now gone,
Some lying next, others not.
Cold marble holds short legends, dates
For grinding wind, rain, snow, ice to erase.

Winter, Late

As evening falls and the last breath of day fails,
And forms around me merge with shadows,
I feel a sorrow as of one deserted
Who has worn the promise of time given
And mourns that it will come no more,
And all that shone in morning sun
Has weakened, gone grey and paled.
I feel a cold breath pass through me.

Grey geese have clattered across the sky,
Homeward going to a black reservoir
Below violet steeping hills.
Deer have started in the pine forest,
Seeking matted paths worn in foreboding hours.
A cloud-covered moon veils toilers in the dark.

Dream Tide

Dreams flood in all through the night
As from a gate lowered.
An insistent tide scours deep and wide
To wash up on a battered shore
Long-held desires and stifled cries,

And in the foam are scattered
Wind-blown archaic leavings,
Residue of shelled creatures
That hide in sand below the surf.

Leaping dolphins stream and lead a boat,
Scudding on the surface of a bay,
Whose rudder fractures waves
When waking strictures do fervent battle
Against the force of night.

Silver Morning

I watched the silver morning fall,
And soon a rose ball arose,
Climbed the farther fence
And paled in colorless day.
Meanwhile, the moon held sway,
Monarch of a draining sky,
In branched spikes of trees.
A weakened glow soon gave way,
Receded, farther seeming, faded.
Pallor encompassed the day,
Foreboding the grasp of care,
Depleted when last lights
In other people's houses waned
Against the demands of day.

Branches

They mirror the wind
And ride rough tides in the sky.
They are pulled and shaken, hauled.
The wind grabs and claws.
Limbs are flung upon currents and sprawled
Against a vast emptiness of clouds.
Grey, an unseen sun withholds
Showerings of gold.
What fierce blows branches endure
Through wavering arms!
What ripped leaves are torn
Living from their holds?
What birds are sheltered,
Hidden and trembling?

Niobant

I saw a weeping woman, silent,
Shoulders rocking, like a small child,
Her breath in spasm
As though the soul within her,
Withering, beat on bars for escape.
What sorrow rules her heart or bows her head
I do not know, but despair is the grave
Of dissipated hope-
What loss, what longing crushed,
What tended sapling snapped,
What bone, what love embraced,
What expectation gone?
Her grief is too deep for word or sound,
Eternal, weeping mother of the world.

Damascus Road

I.
The winter sun slices the sky
Into swords of light that blind
A rider or driver as though behind
Looms inescapable darkness
Unless a portal is made
By an opening of thought
Through a morass of doubt.
The fettered binds of troubled years,
The worrisome titles of old fears,
The unfilled longings of starved desires
Lead to a paring away, to hoofbeats or tires
On a sandblasted roadway
Of stolen sight toward an inward lightness
Through a clouded mirror to brightness.

II.
Into that light is the blinding
Against the reeling of shadows,
Specters of failed promises
Or burnt stars in unrelenting skies.
From the rubble of misplaced hope
That pales the willingness to trust
A new figure emerges
Through a splitting of sky.
Another traveler is revealed,
In voice sensed or heard in whining tires.
A spirit crushed, an aura hushed,
A rider is felled by the edge of truth,
In the plodding of ancient hooves
Toward a tomb or garden grove.

Birthday

The robin sings loudly,
Insistently of the spring
Before I rise on the morning
Of my birth, again.
In degrees of belief in song,
I stir and count seeds of hope.
The bird does not eat grains I leave.
Instead, it sings full-throatedly,
Demanding the air
Bear its prayer to the morning
In the still-cold break of day
When the sun is yet a mystery,
And the night has grown old,
Waning that the day may unfold.

White Violets

In courses of the night
When dreams or torments rule,
And dead hopes are silent visitors
That steal between belief or doubt,
Between raw-edged petals and torn leaves,
Old loves rise in scraps of pain;
Sentinels keep watch, unexplained.

Night lights beckon and reclaim
A shade of peace from keening birds' songs
Long hours before the dawn
Casts feathers on the ground,
And eyes grow lightened in the dark.
White violets absorb faint light.
Rain rustles the edge of night.

Before Dawn

As night is paling
And hope of day returns
Bleakness fades to silver
Before the dawn
Is gilded by the sun,

Before the crush of birdsong
Crowds the fragile morning
Or paces away the hush,
Before feathers rustle
Or wings beget a rush

In a moment of suspended breath
An opening in the sky
Looses rose and yellow
And suffuses land and water with a glow.

Night Light

The light that had opposed the night
Is diminished, paled
To a small spot, a remembrance
Or lost token, a guidance revoked
In the flooded arc of day
That obviates the ache
For protecting walls, moats
To repel demons lurking
In feudal castles of the mind.
Archaic beings, confused between
The sleepful or the real,
People the mind roaming in darkness
And rise in panicked dreams,
Restrained in the night light's beam.

In That Hour

In that hour when night birds
Have ceased their songs,
And those of the day have yet to cry
While darkness still reigns,
When the hush is hallowed
And seems of infinite regret or infinite gain,
The breath of earth rises
In dews or mist or fog
Upon plains or breaches of the forest
Where huddled creatures lay,
And in that time an opening
Of losses or of hope,
A sorrow with shadowed leaves
Is suspended as they breathe.

Grey And Still

Grey and still the morning fell
In dim respite from the dark
Frost upon the earth.
The dawn, steel-hued and grim,
Consumed the bitten scraps of night.
An uncertain sun threatened to obscure
The waif-like castles of dreams
Borne on sleep or memories
Half-retained, half-changed
In the flight of ashen crows
Whose feather warriors
Stormed moats of ancient dread
Of longings composed,
Half sensed, half known.

Yellow Leaf

A yellow leaf
Strung below a bough,
Tethered by a spider's care,
Bespoken by a wind in tones
For a tongue of aging bones-
Leaf- desperate if it had a will,
Fearful if it had a heart,
At danger if it strove to live,
Tormented if it had doubt,

Instead, it sways in current
Of late summer dry heat,
A presage of banishment until spring
Or merely a token of careless blowings
At risk of bird wing crossing.

Section Seven

Pirates

Introduction to Section Seven: Pirates

This is a love story and playlet in verse. Do any of the
characters remind you of someone you know?

Cast of Pirates

Pirate Pilpher, Captain
Leh Mea Doonegan
Dysen Hackett
Murdo MacVincit
Billy Blather
Pud Mudder
Stubb Pegleggin
P. Stolero
Lammen Tibble
C. R. Moonglow
Hamm Merman
Lick'n Stepp
Rowen Orre
O. Penn Hatch
Tar Tom Feather Fled The Heather
Lune R. San Itee
Doyle E. Tatt
Fearce O'Piercy
Phil Landrin
Wyley Justice
Ike N.Guttim
Rolly Stuje

Seafaring Animals

Parrot
Snake
Cat
Monkey
Mice
Goat
Rat

The Ship

Introduction by Pirate: Billy Blather

You'll hear from me, Billy Blather,
Before our time is finished
So loosen your hammocks,
Make pillows of your britches
And listen to our company,
Mongrels of the sea,
Culled from gutters everywhere
The winds and ropes are able to drag us.
Nothing that we do is noble.

My story is much like the others.
I like piracy and the freedom of the sea,
The thrill of thieving
The treasures of others.
It is more exciting than honest work
Of which I've done little.
Jobs are dull and boring
And unrewarding.

It is not a puzzle
Why I am here.
I like the blast of the muzzle
Of cannon and pistol
And being the victor
And fear in the eyes of the loser.
Shall I dispatch him to his fate
Or let him live another day

The Pirates' Song

Lift the fish and let him fly.
Aim your cannons at the sky.
All your treasure lies within
A golden, silver-laden brigantine
Where hurricanes have done our work
And saved us from fire and smoke
And danger to win our prize.

Never doubt your fondant dream
Of castles and rum machines.
Rubies, pearls the oysters know
All can be found below
Where scabbards rust
And mussels grow,
And nothing ever turns to dust.

So lift the fish and let him fly.
He'll show you where the dolphins hide
In hoards of stolen property
Where emeralds and sapphires wink at you,
Where taffy rays come oozing through
The coral reefs to diamond deeps,
Where mermaids have gone to sleep.

So lift the fish
And down your grog.
Mend your sails and tie your knots.
The wind will carry us
And be our chariots
Upon the waves that welcome us.

Pirates' Chorus

Rum and guns,
Pistols and cannon,
Shattered masts
And burning sails,
Falling spars
Or nights of thousand stars
Light the sparks within our hearts.

The winds are fickle
Like round-heeled ladies.
The work is hard, and rewards are scanty.
Stale biscuits crack our teeth.
The ship leaks beneath our feet.
We plug and tar and pump and bail
And raise or lower sails
For rum and guns,
Our faithless mistress
Who laughs at us
And gives us blisters.

The whip and lash,
Keel-hauling and yardarm hanging,
All fearsome things are known to us.
Planks have borne our brothers
To where sharks await a feeding.

So scrim your tusk
And patch your britches.
The ships a jealous mistress,
Second only to the sea
That demands fidelity.
Shattered hearts and skewered dreams
Sink beneath unfathomed deeps
That wash them clean.

Pirate Pilpher, Captain

These unruly men,
Cut throats, bullies and knaves of treachery,
Mercenary to the core, short on mercy
And long on thievery,
I must tame them to my will
And keep them subject still.

If I lead them not to jewels or plunder,
Mutiny will be my fate,
If I cannot intimidate
Or fire imaginations of booty
Beyond the next horizon.

Though winds and currents do not obey me,
I must dominate,
Single-sighted, sure of purpose,
And not tolerate questioning.
Leniency is seen as weakness.
One less is more
Treasure for the rest.

For becalmed or idle they grow surly,
And their mood goes threatening.
Like a storm-darkened sky,
Rampage is in their eyes.
Revenge excites them more though it leads to gore.

From the yardarm dangling
I'll dance my last command.

Pirate: Stubb Pegleggin

Too grand was I in my youth
To heed the preacher's teaching.
I strutted on the rolling decks,
Gallant to behold in cockade hat
And ostrich plume,
With chains of gold
And pockets heavy with doubloons,
But rum and time and feats of battle
Have worn me to a nub
Devoid of glory
The younger men deride and call, "Uncle Peg."

If my tales do not amuse them,
They slap me on the shoulder
To tip me over.
They hide my crutch and watch me scramble,
A clawless crab helpless on the deck,
And if I win at gambling,
They dare me to claim my share.

These men are no kinder than cannon balls,
Nor are they prone to clemency.
Even ladies taunt and call me, "Half-Able."
So bald and lame,
Growing weaker with paling eyes and failing ears,
I spin out stories,
But if I run out of tales
They'll hurl me to the hungry sharks
Without a rub of conscience.

Pirate: Doyle E. Tatt

I would not plow
Or toil at the mill or looms.
I fancied scarlet velvet frockcoats
With cuffs and ruffs of Holland lace
And striped pantaloons.
A pirate I spied in a tavern
Bore a brace of gold-graven pistols.
I put my "X" to sign aboard
For my share of treasure
And adventure,
My saber for a soulmate.

Pirate: Tar Tom Feather Fled The Heather

Hills of heather could not hold me.
Sleeping on my highland plaid,
Cold-bottomed in the dew,
Taught me to flee
The clutch of poverty
And the raiding of the cattle
Until one laird condemned me,
But the pointing of my snee
Through his brass-buttoned heart
Brought me relief
And set me free
To find riches
The world owes to me.

Pirate: Rowen Orre

I labored seven years
For the father of my lover.
He promised me his daughter
Until a wealthy man paid
To have her as his mistress
And not a bride.
She lacked a dowry
Though she was rich in beauty.

When I stole her, she wept
And escaped back to her father.
I fled the Crown's justice
To steal the ships of gold laden with taxes.
Her face haunts me
In every shining doubloon
And every clouded moon.

Pirate: Lune R. San Ittee

Some say the moon is far and distant,
Cold and unavailing,
But I have heard its urging
Away from trees or cliffs that hide it
To the open water
Where it dances in the currents
Or veils itself in clouds.
Those who mock me perish.

Pirate: P. Stolero

Guns have been my friends,
Caressed in the hand,
And flaming trouble for those who cross me.
Each small explosion of powder and flint,
Pellets that storm the heart
And lay it bare,
Release my lust
For what is just
And, for me, fair.

Pirate: Lammen Tibble

I loved a lord's daughter
And she loved me
As I blew upon a trumpet
To announce him at the gate.
He would have me manacled
For loving above my station.
I fled to the port
For the king's navy.
I sought shelter in a tavern
Where the toasts kept flowing,
And I woke on a pirate ship
With a bounty on my head
Though I had done no wrong.

Pirate: C. R. Moonglow

Though I have harpooned whales,
I found it a dirty, smoking business
Of guts and blubber.
These noble creatures
That protect their young
Glared at us with fixed eyes
While we dismembered them
As if it might provoke our caring.
I swore they did not deserve this fate,
But my fellow men, savages all,
Deserve what they get
From the sharp end of my sticker.

Asleep in my berth,
I sometimes see ghostly whales afloat.
They whistle songs to me
That torment my reverie
And call me to join them
In the foam.
And when they turn, I feel that ghastly eye
Goring me.

Lady Pirate: Leh Mea Doonegan

My black locks ,
Scented of lilacs and the dawn
Hide one side of my face.
My father cursed me for his half-pocked beauty
And mark of his disfavor,
A burden no man would wed.
He blamed me for my mother's passing,
Claimed by sickness for tending me.

Alone but for the warm-breathed cows,
I sang until a man lured me from the milking stool
When I clung for a cup of love,
And the daughter I bore
Drew never a breath.
I buried her under a weeping yew
Where no man could ever betray her.

I fled to the rocking arms of the sea
And the taking of treasure,
My sword as sharp as any man's,
And the rage in my heart makes me stronger.

Pirate Rolly Stuje

Too dumb was I, they said, to churn
A tub of butter.
Huge and clumsy, I could not make my mark
Or count my numbers.
The cobbler had not leather
Enough to shoe my feet,
And so, I wrapped in sacks and rags
In any kind of weather.
They fed me on the pigs' leavings
And laughed at me despitefully,
And when I ate greedily,
They called me, "Pork'n Shoat."

Then one day, my father
Clapped hands on me
And squeezed my throat
Until I could not breathe.
I kicked him and stuck
Him with a pitchfork
'Til the blood ran in his eyes.

I ran for the sea
Where a ship lay nearby
And swam desperately.
I climbed the nets to find myself
In pirates' company.

The maidens of the "Crystal Arms"
Twine my golden curls.
They feed me sweets
And kiss my apple cheeks
Then call me, "Wee Rolly."
It takes the coats of two dead men
Spliced together to cover me
And a barrel collar about my waist
To keep all in its place.

In battle I am sure-handed and vicious.
I strike for every taunt I have endured,
And it's there I make my mark.

Pirate: Phil Landrinn

Ladies found in every port
Have graced me with their company
Until the rum and gold are gone.
Then how they flee from me
As if I were a leper!

A true heart throbs in me
That longs for constancy,
Yet I'd rather try another
In case she is better.

Black-haired, blonde or rampant redhead,
Skin like porcelain or ebony
And thighs like marble or mahogany,
How their charms beguile me!
Why should I love but one
And leave the others lacking?

Pirate: Ike N. Guttim

When I was a lad
We slaughtered hogs,
Hogs of any color.
We hammered their heads
And hung them by their hocks.
We opened their throats that bled
Like wine-tapped barrels.
Then we cut out their guts.
We heeded not their squealing or protesting,
Their flailing or their groaning.

A man is not much different than a hog.

Pirates' Lullaby

Refrain:
Oh, the pirate's life for me!
I am famed in infamy,
And the bounty on my head
Comes due when another rogue in my shoes
Swings for the crimes I've profited.
I cut his tongue so he could not lie,
And I go free
To pillage on the sea.
Oh, the pirate's life for me!

I spend my time
In torrid climes
Where sailfish fly
And lush orchids grow
On trees of carmine roses,
Where tigers prowl
With stripes upon their noses,
Where the croc is king
On watery thrones,
And rotted wrecks
Lie just below
The rippling currents,
And at low tide
Their masts abide
Upon the surface,

Where bejeweled idols
Grin and glare
And menace with their threats or curses,
And dead men's bones
Are heaped on ebony altars,
And skulls of empty eyes
Seem to beg for mercy,

Where diamond crowns
Are crusted round with rubies
And emerald stashes glow
In swamp gas light,
Where rhinos roar
Upon the shore
Or monkeys cheat at cards,
Where parrots squawk
And zebras talk
Of stripes and spices.

Where dueling swordfish play all day
And sunken ships bells toll the hours,
Where flying foxes patrol the skies
And lemurs in the teakwood trees
Leap at moths and beetles,
Where salamanders hide
On shoals of coral reefs,
And mermaids dream
In mangroves,
Where turtles coast
Or dig on beaches,
And lizards stalk poison frogs
Or leeches,
Where oysters offer up their pearls,
Where paradise birds
And peacocks strut,
And baboons fill my trunk
With chains of gold and silver ingots,

Where bees make honey in banyan trees,
And rum is brewed
In coconut shells,
And bananas drop in bunches
Where my frockcoat is royal
Scarlet velvet,
And ladies come in clutches

To braid ribbons in my hair
And call me, "Matchless"
As long as silver clinks on the table,
Where sails are furled,
And ships rock in the harbor,

Where pistols load themselves,
And swords hone their edges,
Where nets retie frayed knots,
Where ostrich plumes fan me
In vanilla breezes,
And mosquitos are banished
Beyond the cinnamon trees.

The Parrot's Song

Parrot: S. Q. Awkright

Refrain:
Mutiny! Macaroons!
Walk the plank-a-roons!
Mutiny! Cameroons!
Shipwreck the deck!

Parrot's Ditty:
Belay me in the sheets
But never in the shrouds.
Toss me bones to grind.
Marrow is quite tasty.
Avast me mutton pastie!
Bananas bathed in Madeira,
Guavas soaked in Jamaica rum
And mangoes in Port wine.
Scotch whisky when I can get it
Puts the shine in feathers!
Oranges are peel-ish.
Coconut is beak-ish.
Dates are waxy meal-ish,
And figs have tiny seed-lets.
They are better than the gold
And savory in the gullet.

When we go round the Horn,
And winds are vicious,
Currents are treacherous,
And Good Hope is forlorn,
I am locked in the hold
With sacks of corn and biscuits.

I bob and sway to a hornpipe
When I've had a bit of liquor.
Though pretty, I may be,
My temper can be testy.
Beware my bite is wicked,
And my claws are bear-ish,
But my handsome neck is small-ish
And makes a tempting target.
So, save me from kestrels and petrels
And other flying pest-rels.
Clew your sails! Water your sheets!
Stiffen them in the wind,
And bow your sprits!

The Ship's Lament

Formerly: "The Honor"
Re-named: "Scourge Of The Seas"

Refrain:
Heavy is the burden of villainy.
It weighs me lower in the water
Than a hold laden with gold.

A noble ship have I been
Of stalwart oaken timber,
Hewn from ancient forests
Where the hart and hind prosper.
I am graced by goodly rigging,
Assiduous in service,
Trustworthy to the helmsmen,
Guided by the stars
Or sails shining in the sun,
I am borne by wind to where the crew
Would have me carry them.

Now my good name is shattered,
And shame is my opprobrium
As I am used in villainy.
At least my name is changed
To cover my dishonor.
The blood of honest men stains my boards.
The figure on the prow
Is carved into a goat!
These knaves and looters will make me
End my days in infamy.
I'll not retire to easy duty.
Cannon and flame will end my season
Of hauling booty.

Farewell to the stars and moon!
The wind groans in my rigging,
Sighing and whispering,
The days of honor lost,
The same waves that carry me will cover me.
My final port will be the bottom.
Unfathomable may be
The turns of destiny that lead to ignobility.
Faithful service does not guarantee
An honorable memory.

Pirates' Barber/Surgeon: Dysen Hackett

Refrain:
I soothe my cares
In tropic climes
Where waving palms
Keep pesky flies
From dropping in my grog.

When I scraped the throats
Of honest men,
They paid with eggs or chicken
Or a basket of herbs for a poultice
Or a bucket of leeches to bleed them,
But the cards and drink
Whetted my thirst for the unknown and forbidden.

My hand grew shaky
And my eye less certain,
So they came to me only
When a bone was broken.
A leg, a jaw, an arm or a burn,
These trials to my discernment
Cut into my earnings.

The landlord took no pity
On my reduced condition,
And I became a roving physician
In bleak or freezing weather,
But the pirates gave me rum and food and room,
More rum and a berth for me and my bag of saws.

I find they are less picky
For how I render treatment.
Complainers and failures go overboard

To dance with Madame Shark.
If I lose at gaming, and they hold me to my debt,
I dig deeper in their injuries
Which makes them more forgiving.

Days in port soon lead
To blisters, sores or oozing pain,
Mementos from the ladies.
I mash up roots and weeds
And sassafras
To keep them going.

These pirates are a clumsy sort,
Prone to falls from rigging,
Sprains, cuts and splinters.
They duel with swords and gunpowder
Which leads to sore affliction.
Ghastly wounds are common condition
For lives on the edge of perdition.

With the poppy, hemp and sassafras
Admixed with chamomile and French brandy,
I keep them lulled and in my thrall.
I bandage, patch and stitch their wayward carcasses
To mend them,
But whatever rots,
I lop it.

Pirate: Murdo MacVincit

Refrain:
Subtlety can be a beast with wings
Or a gracious servant.

To conquer by wit takes no blood or sweat.
The force needed is not muscle, but will.
It is more elegant still than deception
That may be uncovered
By the suspicious or perceptive.

I shrink from discovery through subtlety
Of phrase or opinion,
By words and expressions
That give voice to the wind
Or wings to emotion.
Some might call it manipulation.
Others might name it interpretation,
So that loss may be gain, or gain may be loss.
It depends on the presentation.

A promise, half-given,
Need not be a prison.
The key in the lock
Is perception
Turned by fast thinking
And hints of rewards to be gained
By agreement.

First needed is to ferret out longings
Unspoken,
The aches of the spirit,
And hopes near broken.
Few words never assuring but alluring
And keyed to the needs
Make the mold to be cast
For the key in iron.

Thus doors are opened,
And my will is potent.
For good or ill must be chosen,
But for whose benefit
And to what end?
That is the question.

Snake: Argyle Slimchin

Do not look for me in open places.
I prefer coils of rope, cable or chain
For a shelter.
My motion is hypnotic.
My stare is exotic.
It is a lie that I am coated in slime.

I am a squeezer by nature.
I hunt when I slink.
My tail follows my neck down my spine
In a slithery slingle.

Rats are my prey
Who have little chance
To escape my embrace.
My waggling tongue
Says, "Welcome!
I am never alone for long."

These graceless men who inhabit
The ship feed me fat, gristle or bone.
They are awkward with limbs
That stick in all directions.
Too bad for them that they cannot
Slither when prone.

I laugh at their stumbling
And stubbing of toes and shins.
Their inglorious climbing
On ropes or timber
Reminds me that slithering
In any direction
Is far more refined.

They infest the ship
In disorder and filth.
They howl and snarl
Like mad dogs on a prowl
When a hiss, under the breath
Is more eloquent.

Who could believe they are in charge?

Cat: Narcissus Speaks In The Royal We

I speak for my kind.
'Though some besmirch our name,
We are justly famed
As vermin ridders
When we bestir ourselves.

If disturbed in our nap,
We respond with claws
Or a nip on the knuckles.

We don't ask for love.
The right sort of food and shelter
Is enough, that and a sunny window or shelf.
Don't disturb us when we are sleeping.

If we rub your leg
To claim you from others,
Do not give yourself credit
When we deign to accept
You as a servant.

If you are useful, we'll acknowledge you.
Otherwise we'll ignore you.
Don't chase us for affection.
We do not dispense it
Except as a reward.

Humans are so easily manipulated
There is no sport in it
Unless we are bored.
At least mice are more interesting.
Their futile struggles against us
Can be entertaining.
Watching the doomed can be amusing.

Why should we work to provide
When humans will do it for us?
They are readily coaxed
By the hoax of affection.

Do not imagine you are worthy
Unless you serve a purpose.
We tolerate humans
Because they are useful.
They are readily ruled, fooled and cajoled
By a lick or a rub.

Our true task is self-indulgence
And learning to luxuriate
In boredom.

A meow is a snicker
Of our displeasure.
It means you are failing your task.

Conscience would be a tiresome onus
On my magnificent back.
There is nothing diverting
In carrying that burden.
Fortunately, it is something I lack.

Escape Plan For Leh Mea And Murdo

Refrain:
Sand in the hourglass
Is slower running
Than our lives.

Old age is unlikely for pirates.
A bad end is common:
A sword to the heart,
A blade to the throat,
A gun to the gut,
Tropic fevers or bad water,
Tavern brawls and falls from spars,
Overboard in roaring storm,
Mutiny, madness or justice.

Murdo:
Can you not see anonymity
On a verdant island
Would slow our time
To a longer pace
While we try love's charms?

Leh Mea:
How can you love a face such as mine?

Murdo:
I see your beauty side,
But I would cage the beast of rage,
The henchman's heart within you.
Love may gentle you
And belie the scarred half of your face or nature.
Constancy may disarm you.

Leh Mea:
Who says I should be disarmed?
Let four-armed demons try!

Murdo:
I hope this tiger can be declawed!
The small boat on board, the "Omnia,"
I have stocked with purloined stores
To supply us.
When we near an uncharted shore,
We'll steal into a misty night
When the moon will not betray us.
Their rowdiness on board will muffle our splash.
Our oars will cut like a blade through velvet.
We'll row and fly with a darkling sail
That the friendly night will hide.

Together:
All that's needed is the will
For further adventure still
To carry us to the shore.

Leh Mea:
It is true my sword arm may fail
Or my aim tremble over time.
I could bring the blades,
The pistols and powder.
Would that I could carry a cannon!

Together:
We could try our fate
And create a life together.

Leh Mea:
But will we tire of monotony
Or monogamy become a bore?
We'll have only tameness to talk of
Without raids for sport?

Murdo:
Not if I can fill your heart with kindness.

Leh Mea:
That is a stranger I have yet to meet.

Murdo:
Then let me turn that stranger
Into a friend.

Leh mea:
And what if you grow cruel to me?

Murdo:
We'll keep that boat in a hidden grove,
Ready for you,
But how do I know you will not abandon me
If your rage for raids grows?

Leh Mea:
You don't. If I try your fantasy,
You may need to let me go.

Murdo:
Cruel can be the wayward heart,
Fond of inconstancy.
Yet I would not keep you prisoner,
Bound to me by chains of hate.
I would not be a jailor
For the jailed of heart.
If you leave me, regret
May become your burden.

Kindness, respect, then love will be the chains
That bind us.
Magnanimity breeds satisfaction.
Meanspiritedness breeds disrespect,
Hate and revenge.

Leh Mea:
I'll try your plan if I bring
The blades, pistols and powder,
But how can we, only two,
Lacking a crew,
In a boat so small,
Steal cannon and ball?

Murdo:
We'll not need them.
We'll make an eden
With neither cannon nor serpent.
Come let us join hands
And stain them no more with blood.

Leh Mea:
Will this be a ghost
Of the life we've had?

Murdo:
We'll talk of past sorties
In glowing stories,
As we warm ourselves by a fire.
We'll weave palm hats and mats
And build a hut from timber and vines.
When there are storms, we'll shelter in caves
And emerge to see peace on the waves.

We'll plant a garden from seeds I've stolen
To feed us and our children.
They will gladden your spirit
And distract you from sorrows persistent,
'Though old and distant.
Guilt is the ghost you trap in your soul.
You may relent in years well spent,

And one day you may consent
To burn that old boat
Rotting away.
Over the years,
Our time will ripen in a tale
We take pride to tell our children.

Monkey: Me Lee

Refrain:
Boredom is a tiresome thing.
Days are long when the sea is empty.
Trees are more fun than sails or rigging.
Bark to peel and leaves to grind
Are a better use of monkey time.

I ride on the goat
And pull the hair of her poll
And chew on her horn nubs
To be maddening.
When she throws her head and stumbles,
I laugh and chatter and grin,
And then I pick her fleas.

I jump from her back at the parrot
Who shrieks in alarm and displeasure
When I pull his tail feathers.
The snake makes an "S" and hisses.

I spit bananas and steal their lunches.
When a pirate swipes at me,
I nip him and jump on his head
And wrap my tail 'round his neck.
When he pulls it, I bite his ear.
I lost the tip of my tail
In another misadventure.

They tried to pen me in the hold
Where no light or air can enter.
I lured the mice to gnaw the door
Where the hinges are.
As it thundered to the floor

In the echoing hold
Of coffee sacks and betel nuts,
Barrels of flour and beans,
I cocked my head and listened.

The pirates all running
Came fearing disaster.
I threw corn in their faces
And raced to the top of a mast.

There must be something better
To ease my boredom.
I'll rip a sail
And weave it into a curtain.
I'll unbraid a rope
To make a wig
Like ones the judges wear
And a robe from the captain's coat.

If he's drunk, he'll think it fun
And chase me round the cabin.
I'll dump his rum on charts and maps
'Til pirates come with nets,
And the cook chases with a cleaver.
The captain will shout and swear and trip on laces,
All of them with red faces.
They may threaten monkey fricassee
But only if they can catch me.

Mice: The Pink-Toed Victors

We scurry and scamper
In larder or hamper.
We forage on biscuits and leavings.

It is a fiction that our predilection
Is only for cheese.
We eat grain or melons or rice,
Wheat ears or corn or limes.
Our taste is wide-ranging,
Our appetite ceaseless,
Our family innumerable,
Our breeding indefatigable,
A superior species, undefeatable.

We may gnaw through barrels of oak.
The unwary among us may drown in wine.
Wicker is easier and less challenging
For teeth ever lengthening.

We shelter in bedding, boots or old sacks.
We thrive in disorder.
We scatter at trouble
And regroup in a huddle.

Lucky we are
There is no owl on board,
But if ever there was a nemesis
It is cats.

Vain and aloof,
Sneering through whiskers
And up-curled lip,
Soothed by self-licking
Or napping in sun,
Indifferent to opinion,
Entitled and overweening,

Ice-hearted and cruel,
Amused by tormenting others,
If demons have doubles,
They are cats.

Goat: Ghillie Cuddudder

Refrain:
The wind from the mountain,
The breeze from the sea
Sometimes carries the scent
From my island home
As if we are nearing reprieve.

They kidnapped me from an island
Of sweetest grasses lush and tall,
Full of the juice of the sun,
Wild roses of the meadow
And berries of vines that twine
And bees that hum amid din-some birds.

The men had come to dig,
To root up the meadows,
Like their brothers, the hogs,
To find or hide their tasteless gold,
But they soon found the true treasure
Was shallow wells of fresh water
And springs hidden in the cleft of boulders.

How I loved my cliff-side home!
Rocky tors and promontories
To leap from one crag to another,
Defying the sliding schist.

Once in their ship, my friends disappeared
Amidst a racket of screaming, squealing, wrestling goats
And laughing men.
A loathsome odor from a turning spit or boiling pot,
Would rise to blight the heavens.
One man soon wore a hairy cap

Smelling of my friend.
Another wore a vest.
What beasts they are to delight
In the suffering of another!

And when my milk runs out,
I dread I will be next,
But fear is worse
Than the knife.

Leh Mea Doonegan Speaks to Murdo

It is said that true love
Is a treasure attained by the few
But longed for by the many.

It is not bought by stolen gold
Or by the silver earned
Or from ships assailed
Or from the cutting of throats.

A stab wound to the heart
Produces only blood
And loss of quickening,
But hearts may die in other ways:
From lack of nourishment by hope
Or lengths of loneliness endured
Or weight of guilt, self not forgiven.

Some may pine for decades
Over a dream never clothed in flesh.
When time sinks below the horizon,
Only then will longing cease
Or when what seems offered
Is shown to be dust.

What would you offer me-
Dreams or dust
Or something I could trust?

Murdo Speaks Of Leh Mea

She is a bold lady
With the heart of a Bengal tiger
And its claws
And the will of an eagle to hunt its fill.

One half of her face
Is pure as sunrise at sea,
But the other is marred
By scars of affliction.

So too is her nature.
She can be tender
Or melancholy as a setting sun
Falling below a darkening horizon
Or cruel as a raging tide
On a storm-torn shore.

She is fierce and fragile,
Strong but scarred,
Able with a sword
But easily wounded by words.

In part, I long for the maiden unspoiled
By disease or betrayal.
She has imprisoned
Or forsworn that girl,
But I see an under-water river
Running at odds with the tide.

Her life may not be long.
Piracy is a young man's trade.
She has already buried her heart
In an unnamed grave
Beneath an ancient yew.

I think she would not have me
If I implored her.
She would not respect
One who would adore her.

I would be seen as weak
Or poor in judgment.
She would shut me out
Rather than trust herself or me.

I have longed for the charms of love
And peaceful years
On a palm-strewn shore.
I doubt she would believe
That pardon or reprieve
Is deserved by her or me.

She sees ugliness in her glass
And no other possibilities.
She does not trust
In love regained once lost.

She does not believe in worthiness
For the one deceived.

Pirate: Lick'n Stepp

I grew up on cobbled streets,
Unwanted and unlettered.
I slept huddled in darkened doorways
And stole crusts and scraps.
'Though I was a beggar
And cried for mercy,
I saw hardness of heart from all
Until I saw a pirate in his finery
With an odor of rum and warmth and gunpowder
Who promised me warmer climes and treasure.

Pirate: Wyley Justice

Flags we keep in a dead man's chest,
Trophies of our pillaging,
And we hoist them as we go,
So they lead like Judas goats
The unwary to our trap.

As we lay beside them,
Supposedly to parlay
We deal them a dire fate.

Beleagered as they are,
We hew down their spars
And chop their masts for firewood.
We leave them forlorn and starving
With not a farthing.

Learn from me:
Trust no one on the sea.
Many are the tricks of infamy.

Pirate: Pud Mudder:

The landlord's fields
Held me captive
To the plow and mud,
The endless sowing
And sweaty reaping
And the grain never our own.
Mired between taxes and famine
And the headman's brutal ways,
I held a baling cord to his neck
And silenced his mouth forever.
The pirates welcomed me,
Freed from mud and slavery,
To their company.
There are no farm fields on the sea.

Pirate: Hamm Merman

At the forge,
I sweated and swore
And cursed the ore.
Hard-cored iron
Was not the lady for me.
Open water and breezes flowing,
No more pounding, no furnace roaring,
No hard working!
That is the life for me,
Taking treasure easily.

Pirate: O. Penn Hatch

My father's harsh piety
Drove me to the sea.
My mother's weeping shamed me.
Her I could not save,
But I would not follow in his course
Of stone-hearted charity.
'Tis better to be a buccaneer
And kill men honestly.

Pirate: Fearce O'Piercy

The blade has always pleased me,
Cold and sharp as a keening gale.
Slitting, stabbing throat or gullet
When red tide starts flowing
Like an algae sea.
How it pleases me in honing, whetting,
Grinding gristle or severing tendon
Or slicing ropes like errant serpents
Wrapped about a tree.
The back of knee
Always brings them down.

The Leaving Of Hamm

The island where we last saw Hamm
Was one of fearful possibility
And fire fiercely bright
Surrounded by an eerie light.
We heard an anvil sound
As of one hammering.

Then sorrow overcame his caution.
Throwing himself overboard,
He swam toward his destruction,
Lured by the sound of hammering.
The sharks got him.

The Rat Song

Rats: L.D. Structor and Lester Infester
Duet

Refrain:
Victory can be a gnawed thing.

We dodge the snake and cat,
Worthy adversaries both.
Although we stow
On boats big and small,
We have no friends on any.
We are able chewers,
Never sea sick,
Persistent and ever-breeding.

We feast on whatever our teeth can grind.
Grow, grow is their habit,
So we must gnaw on, on.
Our pastime is destruction, wanton.

We scatter disease
With our fleas
Wherever ports are distant.
Don't look for us.
We'll find you,
And if you sleep,
Beware your feet.

'Though ignoble and nasty we may be,
We take over on land and sea
And soon populate the ports we dock.
Tight-rope walking on tying lines
Or board-floating on debris,
These are our transports,
Not to mention sacks of grain.

Unwelcome riders we
Pay no fees
But live at ease.

Pirates' Tale

Narrator: Pirate Billy Blather

We left the ports of riotous fun
And maidens of "The Pistol Arms,"
The tavern where we drank our gold
And loves never grow old or cold.

We bashed the stools and cracked the bottles
And gambled on the timber tables,
Relics of lost ships,
Splintered on rocks or shoals.

False lighthouses drew us in
And lured us to our ruin.
Sails became our ragged shrouds
In unmarked graves of infamy.

Silver buckles from our shoes
Became combs in maidens' hair.
Our boots moldered where fishes hide,
And cannons grew barnacles on their sides.

Our treasure gone and we in drunken stupor,
Our captain rowed with pots of gold
Sinking in a leaking hold
Of rotted ship he commandeered

With bows tied in his beard
Roaring at the fools we were
To meet our fate on barren speck
Of land where sea lanes never intersect.

Seagulls mock us with their cries,
And we cursed our destiny
The day the rum ran out.
We took a vote to fire the wreck

To light a warming beacon
Or to patch a raft
With sails of shirts.
An even tally for each course,

We battled with cutlasses and clubs
Then lashed a raft
Of charred timbers
With seaweed ropes and rags.

We cast ourselves upon the mercies of tides
With the sun searing our backs,
The salt parching our tongues,
Boobies diving overhead,

Albatross crying for our loss.
Our rowing brought us no reward.
The tide upturned us
On the shore with only weeds or stones to eat.

Now, I recall our lost glory
And the merchant ships we boarded
While our cannons thundered,
And spars fell like August stars.

All the brave men slaughtered,
We brought their ships under our lee,
 Their guns turned toward the sea,
Or burnt them where they lay at anchor,

But all our struggles came to naught,
All the battles won or fought,
The gales endured and loves lost
For I alone survive

With grinning sharks for company,
Surrounded by ravaged skulls of men,
I ponder the finned devourers
That will bear me to a watery home

Or the birds that will pick my bones.
A pirate's life is grandest fun,
Filled with treasure and adventure
And tales wondrous to share,

Though I will perish with only birds to hear
And waves slapping at my feet,
Scuttling crabs to pinch me where I sleep,
Sand and foam for coffin,
Gulls for mourners,
Cackling.

Section Eight

Leaving the Ark

Introduction to Section Eight: Leaving the Ark

This playlet in verse asks: What was it like to be on the ark, and to face leaving it to enter a changed world?

Leaving The Ark

Refrain:
We are the children of destruction.
How will it settle?
Where will it end?

The world that has been is no more.
The pastures, forests and vineyards are gone,
All swept away in a furious flood
When the Lord turned His face from us,
And we, the creatures who filled the earth
With a living creation song,
Have paid for the wrongs of men.
We are reduced to pairs of our kind
To renew the scourged earth.

What kind of world will it be?
Where will we make our haven?
And what of our children,
How will we raise them?
How will the tender seedlings grow?
Where will the rivers flow
If they have lost their course?
Where are the sheltering trees
And royal crowns of leaves?

And the face of the sun,
Our anchor of gold in distress,
Will it burn us or warm us?
How can we hope for gentleness
In the churning of devastation?

All of us are in need,
The mighty or small,
Those that fly or crawl,

The chewers and gnawers,
The diggers and maulers,
The stalkers and clawers,
The snails and slugs and bugs.
Where will we make our dens and nests
On a barren plain of waste?

We are the maned or striped or spotted,
The finned, the furry, the slimy or bald,
The long-necked and long-trunked,
The horned or hooded or hooved,
The hoppers and prowlers and leapers,
The climbers or creepers,
The twiners and squeezers,
The gliders and sneakers,
The weavers and spinners of nest or web,
The builders of hives or mounds,
Those that burrow or scurry or scuttle
That sidle or spit or flit or glow,

Those that hum or whirr or bellow,
The cluckers and trumpeters and chirpers,
The singers and buglers and croakers,
Those that whinny or hiss or honk or bray,
The crowers and snorters,
The bayers or barkers or yelpers,
The squeakers and squealers,
The whistlers and wailers and whoopers,
The mewers and hooters,
The coo-ers and moo-ers,
The growlers and howlers,
The roarers and those that chatter or chortle,
All are a chorus of works of the Lord,
A mighty harmony,
Attuned to His glory.

The Creator is praised in our being.
We are the seed of His kindness.
Will He abandon us in our need,
Or will He channel the rivers and seas
And hold back the deserts
And give us the blessings of trees?

Will the olive branch in the mouth of the dove
Be a sign of His mercy and peace
To lead us in our release from the ark?

Refrain:
We are the children of need and destruction.
How will it settle?
Where will it end?

Lion

It is written that I
With the meek will lie.
With the Lamb
Will my children abide,
And hay will suffice
When Messiah arrives
As promised,
And we will have peace.

My hide is the color of desert sand,
My mane a cloud of thunder,
My paws for striding,
My claws for striking,
My terrible teeth for tearing.
What a king am I!
But even a king must defer
To the Lowly One
When He arrives.

When I roar through the dark,
Long hours of night,
And the spirit feels worn and forsaken.
Rejoice!
I proclaim the power of the Lord
For a day of great awakening
When all will know,
We are equally blessed.
He never withholds His love,

And the sky and the sea and the earth
Sing praises,
And peace will shower on us
And flowers unfold in the desert
Of the weary spirit, uplifted.

Horse

I'm going to race out of this place
And loosen my legs
For I am made to run.
I'll toss my mane
And chase the sky
And gallop on plains
Where grass grows high,
Wave my tail like a flag
And kick and stamp
And whinny and neigh
My worries away.

When I get out of this place,
I'll kiss the wind
And buck and snort
And dance and prance
Faster and faster
For I am master
And say goodbye to Father Noah.
To thank him for his trouble,
I'll carry his kin on my back.

The wind won't whistle or whisper.
The clouds won't rain for days.
The sun will wink,
But the clouds won't sink
'Neath my horizon.
For this day is my own.

Don Key Brae

My kind are often mocked with in-glory
And treated poorly.
We are constant servants to man
And carry his burdens in humility.

For the perceptive, our braying is speech.
Those who listen may learn,
But lessons spurned profit man not at all.

Someday our lowliness
May be blessed
By a Rider Who calls us His own.

I ask my fellow travelers to speak
And tell us their stories,
Their worries and needs.

Hyena

Don Key Brae:
Even the despised ones
Have a lesson to teach us.

Hyena:
Though I prowl and howl
And laugh at the fearful,
Know that I am no more
Than the terrors of night, revisited,
As embodiment of loss or doom.
My mission shows
That even the low
Have a place in the kingdom,
And the lost will survive
In the mind of the Creator Lord
In some as yet unknown form.
His love endures,
And His energy is never wasted.

Elephant

I rumble and thunder,
Bellow or grumble
And trample the grass to dust.
A cloud I raise in my passage
And uproot trees for fodder
And leave the logs for others to hollow.
Tender am I to the young
And pull them up slippery banks of mud.
We linger with the ailing
And mourn our dead.
We visit their bones to caress them.

The young ones trek between my feet,
Shaded from the sun.
We trumpet water or dust
And wallow in mud to cover our skins.
Our tusks are tools
To uproot trees
Or weapons to protect us.

I have been the servant of man
In war or logging or riding.
The Lord made us mighty but willing.
Who but demons of greed
Would destroy us?

Fishes

Those who listen carefully
May hear our gentle burbling
Or see bubbles break the tension
Of liquid skin
And watch us dart and flick,
Below the surface, quick.

We soothe the watchers
In our flowing
Oneness with the water.
Our tails may thrash
And lash the currents
In spreading circles.
Our movements show
How the water works
To hold us above the bottom
And below the surface,

Or in the darkest deeps we glow
Far below what man may know
Or rule as his hegemony.

Surely He who plumbs the depths
Has set our mystery
And made us bearers of liquid light
That even we need not go lampless
In eternal night.

Cricket

Don Key Brae:
Cricket whirs and chirps
And dances among leaves
And thickets and thistles.
He knows how quickly
Seasons pass
And may know how long
The flood will last.
Listen and let him speak.

Cricket:
Sawing legs have I.
Their rubbing makes a whirring sound,
And so I lead a solo symphony
Of changing seasons.
We stowed aboard Noah's ark
To keep the creatures company
In stuffy, close-held proximity.

When they grow restive,
I quiet their noisy stamping
And bawling, their lowing,
Howling and blowing
So that others may welcome sleep.

I sing them the lore of changing earth
To reassure and comfort them,
And so Noah welcomes us
Among the bales of fodder.

I sing to them of courage needed
To be like our ancients who profited
From gracious earth
By following their better sense

Given by the Lord.
I remind them they, too, will find a home
When the doors are opened.
The dove will lead us
To replenished land,
And as she bears the olive branch,
Peace will be her message.

Tortoise

Don Key Brae:
Hush! Let old, wise tortoise speak.
He is closest to the earth and humble on his belly.

Tortoise:
I have lived long enough to know
The wise are humble,
And the humble of heart are uplifted.
I am not ashamed to be near
The heart of the earth,
Or the ground we will be glad
To see and have under our feet.

It is true I have lived longer than most
And have seen the proud and greedy brought low,
The arrogant of spirit claim all the earth provides
As theirs alone. Now they are fallen.
We creatures may teach them by example
To fill their need
But leave the rest for others.

I have outlived many storms or drought,
The passing of the seasons, ever fleeting,
But never have I seen a flood such as this.
It is a warning to users and abusers
Of Earth that their deeds are counted.
Their wrongs to the Lord, to men, to the earth,
All are counted, the total mounting.

It is true we are the victims of men.
Our task is to show them how we, the brave,
Give our bodies that others may live
And lose our freedom to bear their burdens.

Those who degrade us
Miss the meaning of sacrifice,
And our atonements for their wrongs.

They fail to understand
The dignity of our cause.
We are the first to be wasted
And the last to be missed
When we are gone.
And so we endure
As well as we can
In a world of disorder
Caused by men,

But we must find hope
In this beginning
Of Earth washed clean
And chastised man.

Crow Speaks

I am the darkling,
The cawing one.
Does no one understand my message?
I warn the winged flocks
To beware the hawk who hides in waiting.
I chase the jays
From nestlings or eggs
And warn parents to cover
Their young with wings,

And soon, my tasks I'll resume
When trees are hosting nests.
I'll fly unbound
In fields and forests
That welcome me
And resound with my cawing.

Dolphin

Don Key Brae:
The dolphins still are singing,
Clicking and whistling
In a tongue unknown to men.
Listen that we may learn from them.

Dolphin:
Brother creatures, for we are brothers.
We are one in sharing hearts that beat
And in striving to live long.

The water is joy to me
As I sweep among its currents.
I dive and coast and sail
Like birds who ride the air
Or lightning that triumphs in the skies.

When the seas regain their bounds,
I'll know my proper place to roam
And sing my water song.

Owl Speaks

Hoo Terrie:
Howlers of the savannahs,
Prowlers of the jungles,
Monarchs of the air
Seek a distant forest.

All are on a great migration
Since the inundation
Of the world
Where we knew our places.

I see deeds of the dark
And the moon that caresses
The tips of branches
Or rides in the rippling wings of the sea,
Gliding on the current.

I see the actions of men
Behind the curtain of night
When all darkness
Reveals itself in starlight.

The acts of men
Are known by those
Who penetrate darkness of mind
And see into fires of the heart.
Now all are quenched by the flood.

The difference between creatures
That hunt by night
And men
Is innocence or its lack therein.

We creatures do as we must
But not deeds of darkness of heart.

Mice

Don Key Brae:
Grey is the color of uncertainty,
The vaguely known or sensed or ominous.
Listen carefully! Though his voice is small,
He tells what we all have felt.

Mice:
I speak for my kind and for being little
In a world big and beyond understanding
The intent of many to destroy us,
Where danger lurks
Wherever we turn
And where monsters, like cats, are real.

In hope of reprieve we appeal,
Please save us from the cat,
We squeak and chitter
To Father Noah.
The ark is to be a place of peace
And safety for our number,
But the cat looks bored
And glares at us,
And so we're feeling anxious.
Surely, in the new world
Man will need us
To glean his leavings.

Noah

I stand in the ark,
The tomb of my heart,
Grieved from the losses
Of all that I knew.

This work of my hands,
From the word of the Lord,
Is a womb of remaking,
A journey of souls,
Where the dark unknown
Gives birth to a world made new,
Washed clean of all sorrows and wrongs.

The animals call me Father Noah,
But there is only one Father
In whose shadow I stand.
My family shovels and feeds
And waters His flock
'Til He relieves us of this burden.

We have sacrificed trees for the ark
And seen heartwood weep
Under the blade of the saw,
The grain shatter under the adze.
We have sealed it with pitch
And chinks and tar of despair
In days and nights of wandering
In a watery desert,
Our hearts longing for release.

So, we must build in our spirits
An ark to ferry us to Him.

Cat

Snoo Tee:
What a rabble is on board this ark,
Motley, noisy, crowded, rude and stinking!

I keep myself clean and trim
Despite unworthy ones around me.
I should be given
A princely pillow or cushion
Since I am deserving
Of privileged position.

The mice are in havoc
And running for shelter
When I give them my welcoming grin.
By the time we debark,
They may be extinct.
There is little else worth the effort.

Sheep

We have shown men the meaning
Of gentleness and generosity
And given him our fleece and meat.
We have clothed him in
Spun and woven thread.
When we are sheared in ungainly pose,
How near our throats
His clippers go!

We are meek and easily led.
We need a Shepherd
Whom we can trust
To seek us when we are lost.

Our sacrifice is one of blood
That sizzles in smoke and gore.
The perfect among us are chosen
And the poor carcass
Burnt upon altars
To ashes and charred bones.

 In thanks for deliverance
Men will build a new altar,
And our young will end upon it
Until someday when men learn
True sacrifice is in the heart and spirit,
And burning flesh
Brings no merit.

Ox

Our ark is dark
And nurturing like a womb.
'Though we are on a journey,
For us it will end as in a tomb.
We will plod and plow and toil 'til we fall.

Someday we may share a stable
With One yet to be born
On a cold night
With a cold star for welcome.
Our breath may caress
One in need of warming.
He will be humble like the ark,
But He will promise us peace
When the yoke and burden are eased.

Lizard

My checked and dry skin
Wraps about horns or ruffs
Or eye stalks.
My tail swings to balance my stride,
And my marvelous tongue
Snaps and flecks and wags
In a whirry of distraction.

Rocks and sun are my attraction.
Cold and wet are my nemesis.
My cousins grow in colors
Brown or green or blue
In sizes small or huge,
And we alone know whether dragon
Tales are true.

Some of us may seem to fly
Who have mastered gliding.
Our eyes on spikes
May gyrate alarmingly.
Thus we may see
In two or three directions
To search our horizons.

Ever watchful are we.
We teach the need for vigilance
In a world of quickened tongues.

Bee

Storied for our industry,
We are a necessity
To the plants for man to eat.
When we suck nectar,
We spread pollen powder
For plants to share
And bud or blossom or bear their fruit.
Not much will grow without our care.

We build our hives and attend our queen.
We hum and buzz as we work
And tell stories by dancing.
Our legs a-twitter,
We give direction
Where the richest nectar flourishes.

In an environment newly clean,
We will make an Eden,
Freely thriving and green.
We will give men grain to eat
And honey to sweeten
The sourness of sorrow.

Ant

We soldier on in columns unbroken
'Though the big may trample us
Without noticing,
And when order is crushed,
We reform and march.

We chew and ferry
And, staggering, carry
Pieces of leaves
Or debris
Home to our nests.

Man could learn from us:
Diligence is the path to reward.
When we work as one
In singlemindedness,
Never despairing or idle,
We will not be beaten
Nor leave scraps uneaten.
We are cleaners of the earth.

Friend Snail

Some say I am slow and slimy
And leave a trail behind me
No one wants to follow,
But a certain light
Gives my slime a shine
So that it nearly glitters.

Perhaps I have a lesson to share:
Be not too sluggish to learn
An aura or glisten of beauty
Can be found in the humblest trails.

My antennae of twin coronets
Crown my brow
As they point toward the clouds.
They waver in time
To the march of slime
And guide me ever onward.

And what of my castle I carry?
Have you ever seen its match
Of home with escape hatch,
Or trap door to snap safely closed?

Who says that feet are needed
To carry me on my path?
I am gifted with ooze,
Thus I need no shoes.

My slime is fine
To ease my road and the load
As I tarry at a stately pace
And embrace what surrounds me.

Though the proud often fall,
I travel well
With no feet at all
And leave a trace of my way
To remind me
How far I have come this day.

Sister Spider

Don Key Brae:
Let us learn to be fair
And give our sister creature
A chance to be heard.

Sister Spider:
I am despised by many,
But have you not seen
The dew of dawn
Glisten when caught
On my tender threads
Of elegance?

Does no one admire my artistry
Of tethered and netted webs
Spun finer than feathers
And lighter than hair
And all of it
From my abdomen?

I spin and spin and extend my grasp
To make cocoon blankets.
Are there any who could copy me?
My frail-seeming legs,
Each knowing their task,
Work together in unity.

The mighty could learn from me
That a lighter touch
And subtler snare
Have their own utility.
Blundering and heedless brawn
May come to naught but ruin.

Those who would see strength
Look not only on the mighty
But on those who thrive
In fragility.

Hope

Refrain:
The home of clouds is the home of hope.
The earth forgives when men are good to it.

See that river!
See that bounty flowing!
There is hope! There is hope!
The earth is remaking
So that we may partake
Of the riches it offers us.

We may search to find our home.
We have the earth to make our Eden
Where there is room for all
And where we have a purpose.

The deserts may echo in thunder
When the rains flow to enrich it,
And floods find their course.

The heavens have stopped their weeping
For the wrongs of men.
The sun is a beacon,
And clouds are filled with light.

The mountain tops emerge
From the scourge of flood.
Green branches flourish
On the foothills.
There are channels for the river course,
Reeds and marsh appearing.

The earth is clean, daring
To wake again
From the wrongs of men.

A chance! There is a chance
To restore our Eden,
And we may have peace
Upon the land and sky and water.

All

In our days and nights of dark confinement
We have learned to tolerate
Differences anchored in respect
For Him who has saved us
And sent the dove,
The olive-branch bringer,
As messenger,
And emblem of our Comforter.

In harmony that sweetens the air
The Creator may hear
With a diviner ear
A song in our cacophony.
He sees through the core
Of planets and into the depths of souls.
His voice is in the roar
Of waterfalls and volcanoes.
His whisper shivers the tree limbs
And bends saplings to His will.

Like lava His foot strides on new land
That glows orange and smoking
In the breath of creation
And foments the oceans
In agitation.
His storms chasten the waves.
His sorrows, like sand,
Envelop the roots of plants
In searing aridity.
All exist in a power
We do not understand.

In His hands our ark
Is cradled, rocked on a flooded sea.
We give thanks for His mercy
That has made us a legacy
For those who will come to be
Images of His creativity.

Dog

Our song would be long
To tell all we do for man,
But if we choose one,
It would be as friend
Like no other
Except perhaps his mother.

We generate joy
In the human heart
When we greet our master
Ecstatically.
We assume humble ranks
And presume no duty is owed to us.

We are always true
And grateful
For the smallest boons.
We give warmth and comfort
But ask for nothing
More than a pat or a rub.
For a drink of water, a scrap of food
We give wholehearted return in love.

We love equally the unworthy, the ugly,
The disordered and forlorn,
The treacherous or indifferent.
We forgive cruelty and neglect
Easily and with no regret.
We are models for the better side of man.
In the shadow of the Comforter
Stands the dog.

Flip, The Frog

How we enliven ponds
In mass unity
Of croaking songs,
Raucous and calling
For our kind to decode
A meaning
No one else needs to know!

Flicking tongue
And bulging throat,
Marvels of murky beauty
And buoyancy are we

Who beguile the water
With our kicks!
Humans, though slow to learn,
Strive to imitate our swim.

Have you seen our lithesome
Legs, lean, long and muscular!
Watch us when we hop!
We're gone!

Butterfly

Monarch or moth,
I am blue, yellow, orange or black,
Spotted or lined,
Iridescent or dull,
Fragile but long traveler,
Fleeting in spirit or soul,
Free or netted,
Wild or bred,
A gift or blest,
Weightless delight
Alighting or flighting,
Treasure on wing,
Antennae trembling,
Skipping in air
Then vanishing.

Noah's Three Sons, Shem, Ham and Japheth And Their Wives

Our journey is wearisome,
Our chores never done.
We hope for relief
And to find a new home
Since all that we knew is gone.

For us, the ark is bastion
And prison, a testament
To Noah's wisdom
Given to him
From beyond our vision.

How unlike a garden
Is a ravaged earth
Depleted, made poor,
Stripped of potential
With little left for taking,
A scourged planet
Punished like an errant mother
Who has given birth and nurture
To plunderers!

How like a waterfall, ever-streaming,
Have been the blessings
Showered on us by the Lord!
Now our future is uncertain,
Our blessings scorned,
A cataclysm needed
To teach us our errors.
Will the next generations learn?

Chicken

A venerable creature am I!
Some say we have conquered the earth.
We are plentiful
And spread across lands.
My eggs and flesh feed the many,
But often I am treated cruelly,
Close-penned in disgraceful captivity.
Humble but fighting in spirit are we
Who survive and breed.
Proud rooster struts and wakens all
With his insistent call
Even before the sun rises.
We cackle and cluck and preen and pick.
We sit our nests diligently
Then gather our chicks
Under our wings tenderly
To warm and protect them dutifully.
Models of feathered excellence are we!
How could man do without us?

Cow

Give me fodder,
Or better,
A sunny green hillside
Damp from morning mist,
And I am content
To be grazing or lazing
On a blessed day
When air stirs in a brief caress.

Then, anyone can see how
It is good to be a cow
With a clear stream nearby
And tender leafage easily nipped.

Thus, I am at peace,
Chewing my cud,
Dreaming little
And pondering less,
'Til I return to the barn
For a night's long rest,
And the hay in the loft
Smells of summer.

Kangaroo

This I recall
From the depths of my stall:
Boxing and hopping,
Grazing on plains
Or lazing in shade
Of a welcome tree.

My pouch is a house
Or a baby's cradle,
Warm and safe,
Always available
Like Father Noah's faith.

My tail is a rudder
To keep me in balance
When I bound along my trail.
Big feet are a must
As I bounce through the dust
To lift me in powerful thrust.

The world is amiss
When I'm locked in a pen
In a rolling boat
Under ever-darkening rain.

I must learn to hope
As we keep afloat,
Safe on the ark
Through sunless days
And moonless dark
To wherever our journey ends.

Rhinoceros

Some say I am beastly
Because of my horn
And great size
And armored hide.

It is true I may charge
When I roam at large.
I get testy when pestered
By those who are after my nose.

My toes churn up dust
In my lunging thrust.
My snorting is warning
When I chase interlopers away.

The birds on my back
Are welcome riders.
They can attest to the rest
I am a peaceable neighbor.

I would rather be grazing
And left to myself,
Nipping bushes and tufts of grass.
Vegetation, not confrontation,
Is what I crave.

Eagle

Imperious and above remorse,
In aerie aloft
I raise my young
And feed them on my catch.
In torque of wind
I spin and hurtle
Toward earth or water
Where few escape my clutch.

Rampant and fearsome in the sky,
I remind that clear sight
Is a gift from on High,
But, unlike Him, merciful
I am not.

Tiger

Striped and stealthy am I
With golden stare ablaze
And lips that curl
Over fangs of fury
In a rage and marvel
Of terror and beauty.

I steal on pads silently
Through brush or reed.
In mottled sun or shadow I lurk
To emerge, ears pressed flat, and snarl
At the doomed and hapless
I throttle.

I enrapture them
With my splendid coat
Licked by orange fires
Glowing on my sides
Between blackened bars of ash.
I am tinged with flames of destruction.

Giraffe

The rafters are too low
For my head.
My legs are too long
For my chin
When I'm boxed in a narrow pen
Where I snatch some thatch for nibbling.

Noah warns me not to eat the roof
Or we may sink from rain.
I know he speaks truly,
But I get unruly
When I'm lonely for trees and plains.

My neck is getting a bend,
And thatch scratches my ears.
My knees knock the walls,
And my tails drums the door
As my hooves thump the floor.

I need to stalk the savannahs
For patches of trees with high-hung leaves
And give my neck a stretch,
Let the grass brush my skin
And the sun warm my back
And my stride open wide in the morning.

The Creatures Complaint Chorus

All can be quarrelsome neighbors:
Rhino with his horn
And inclined to charge,
Stag with his antlers,
Badger feared for her temper,
Elephant with her tusks.
Alligator's slapping tail
Alarms boa who constricts in tight quarters,
And anteater snuffles in corners.

The ibex or oryx or spiral-horned eland
All could stick us or gore us.
The horse bucks and kicks.
We have biters or snappers like turtle
Or spitters like cobra
Or the shark's fearsome snout.
Our voyage is perilous,
But Noah is patient and reassures us
'Though he keeps us penned every day.

This is a trying task
As some of us get testy or bored.
Skunk lifts her tail in warning,
And porcupine aims his quills.
Llama and camel hurl saliva.
Armadillo curls in a circle,
And ostrich buries her head in hay.
Butterfly tries to calm
By dancing in air.

Vulture scrapes his beak
And looks hopeful
If anyone sleeps.
When bear hones her claws,

Otter escapes through bars.
Orangutan swings from rafters and thatch.
The termites' chewing may sink us!
The bees may sting us!
Mosquitos drone and 'possum wobbles.

Magpie chatters and scatters
The scraps she finds into hiding places.
Giraffe is lofty in manner.
Flamingos and pelicans dredge the pool
Where penguin eyes the fish.
To shrimp's chagrin, dove mourns her loss.
Macaws and jackdaws are cross.
The eels are uneasy,
And squid squirts ink.

What a relief it will be
When we are set free!
When the plank is let down
And resounds on firm ground,
We'll uncover our ears
And crawl or slink
From nests of straw,
Then crow's loud cawing
Will tell us when to go.

Meanwhile there is racket-some rooster
Who won't let us sleep,
The lion who frightens with midnight roar
And startles the deer to panic.
The pig snorts and grumphs.
The chicken chitters,
And snake rattles.
Coyote cries her care to the moon,
And loon pines an eerie song.

Crickets saw, and toad the tuneless
Warfles a throaty rasp.
Mockingbird mimics a bugling elk.
Sea lions bark, and duck quacks.
Gorilla drums on his chest.
Buffalo beats time with his hoof.
The cow moos, and cranes whoop.
Toothsome tiger grins and growls
As baboon howls and raccoon prowls.

Why can't the owl hoo-hoo in daytime?
Through the long nights, hyena's wild laughter
Prickles the spine and raises the scruff.
Elephant trumpets displeasure.
We grow tired of each other.
Monkey's thieving and teasing does not amuse.
The troublesome set us to stamp or bellow or roar.
Longhorn tosses her head without warning
And beats on the beams.

Burro brays in our ears.
Panda squeals for bamboo.
Ocelot counts spots, and blue jay screeches.
Goose honks and hisses and nips the moose.
Kangaroos and wallabies box.
Lamb bleats and frolics and gambols on bales.
Lobster duels, and scallop scoots loose.
Clam slams her shell shut.
At least the fish are quiet!

Our ark pitches and rolls
In wind or flood.
How much longer, we wonder,
Must we endure?

Where Shall We Go From Here

Now home is lost
Where shall we go from here?
Shall we wander
Alone, bereft of mountains,
Meadows and forests,
The rivers and rocks of our own?
Will the deserts feed us
Or give us shelter?

Where are the trees to climb
Or leaves for cover?
Shall we trek or fly,
Having no place to perch or hide?
How many days for sweet water,
How many nights with the wind
On our hides or feathers
Must we endure?

Father Noah has ferried us
To new lives in new lands
Cleansed of the evils of men.
'Though now we perch perilously
On the crest of a mountain,
We must trust in the Father
Who makes the rain
To send us a Pathway, a Savior.

Our wait will not be in vain.
When Messiah comes,
Rains will replenish the spirit.
Old deserts will bloom
In the hearts of men.
Souls that have withered
Will rejoice in Him.
Winds and tides will obey His command.

Sins of men will not cost us our homes.
Hope and flowers will cover the earth.
Great springs of love will well from the core.
His love will crown the mountains
And beam from the eagle's eye.
Rains will flood the spirit with joy,
And all will sing in wondrous cacophony.

About the Poet

Carolyn Anderson London, LCPC, MS, BFA, lives in the Baltimore metropolitan area. She attended Loyola University Maryland and Maryland Institute, College of Art, as well as Johns Hopkins University.

She has worked as a mental health therapist for inmates in an adult detention center, in outpatient drug and alcohol treatment, in partial hospitalization and in private practice.

Her mother shared the love of poetry by reading aloud the great poets as well as nonsense and children's poems.

Made in the USA
Columbia, SC
27 August 2018